Whispering Death

Whispering Death

THE LIFE AND TIMES OF

Michael Holding

BY

Michael Holding

with Tony Cozier

ANDRE DEUTSCH

First published in Great Britain 1993
by André Deutsch Limited
105-106 Great Russell Street, London WC1B 3LJ

Cataloguing-in-publication data for this title
is available from the British Library

ISBN: 0 233 98828 9

Phototypeset by Falcon Graphic Art Ltd
Wallington, Surrey
Printed in Finland by
WSOY, Finland

To my parents
Ralph and Enid Holding

CONTENTS

ILLUSTRATIONS

CHAPTER 1

A quite special over

They were everywhere, crammed into the limited stands, precariously perched on galvanised roofs, spilling on to the boundary's edge. The 15,000 or so people squeezed into the limited facilities of Bridgetown's Kensington Oval buzzed in excited expectation. They had seen their West Indies team bowled out by England for 265 early that March day in 1981, the second day of the third Test, and were confidently waiting for their four fast bowlers to strike back.

As we went through our final preparation in the confines of the dressing-room in the Pickwick pavilion, our captain, Clive Lloyd, tapped me on the shoulder and asked: 'So which end do you want to come from, Mikey?' It was the first time I'd ever been offered the choice and I wasn't prepared for it. Andy Roberts had always bowled the opening over. 'Whichever end Andy doesn't want,' I replied. To me, there was no question that Andy should bowl the first over, as he always did, but by the time Clive tossed me the ball to start the second over from the northern end, with the George Challenor Stand at my back, I was chafing at the bit.

As usual, Dennis Waight, our trainer, had had us all stretching and loosening up before start of play. I'd been out in the middle for a brief spell with the bat and felt confident. I was fired up by the crowd, by the challenge our modest total had set us, and by

1

the captain's instructions. 'I want you to bowl flat out from the start,' he said. 'Don't worry, I'm only giving you three or four overs, so let's have all you've got.'

Kensington, with its pacy and bouncy pitch and its knowledgeable spectators who had been raised on the deeds of the succession of great Barbadian fast bowlers, was one of my favourite grounds. If I needed any more encouragement, it was staring me right in the face for the pitch was like none I'd seen before. Hard, as usual, but covered with a layer of grass, it was bound to be fast as lightning.

Usually, my first task would be to locate a proper line and length, around off stump, keeping the batsmen on the defensive, before increasing pace and experimenting. Now the intention was primarily speed as I ran in to deliver to Geoff Boycott, a perfectionist whose technique and temperament made him one of the finest opening batsmen of his time.

I first played against Boycott on our tour of England the previous summer and quickly found out where not to bowl to him. An exceptionally good judge of line, he would simply leave alone any ball wide of the stumps. It meant pitching as close to the off stump as possible, forcing a stroke and hoping for an outswinger to find the edge. I'd got him nibbling that way at Trent Bridge, and at the Queen's Park Oval in the first Test a few weeks earlier, only for the catches to be dropped. So I was settled in my mind just where to aim.

I knew I had another advantage. It was psychological. Prior to each Test, I liked to chat to the ground curator to find out how the pitch might play. In Barbados Tommy Peirce was in charge of the preparation and he told me a story which indicated that Boycott wasn't in the right frame of mind. He had scored double-centuries at Kensington in the island matches on England's two previous tours in 1968 and

1974 when the pitch was bare of grass and a batsman's paradise. He obviously came expecting a repeat only to find something completely different. Looking at this one on the eve of the Test, he accosted Tommy and asked: 'What's this then? Where's all this green come from?' 'I just told him that grass in the Caribbean is green,' Tommy said. 'He didn't look amused.'

No wonder. He knew it spelt trouble.

So the cards were stacked in my favour as I ran in to bowl my first ball. It landed more or less perfectly, perhaps a couple of inches wide of the off stump, and drew from Boycott a hurried, uncertain prod. Immediately I became even more confident. Everything was right, my rhythm, my delivery stride, my action. It's rare to feel that way from the very start of a spell and each ball of the over did almost exactly what I planned. Twice, as Boycott played, the ball flashed through to wicketkeeper David Murray. Once he was taken on his thigh pad. The fifth ball I dug in a little shorter than the others and it climbed steeply towards his Adam's apple. Somehow, he got the bat up in self-preservation and the ball dropped a couple of feet or so in front of Joel Garner in the gully.

Immersed in the game, I was usually oblivious to the crowd when bowling, but this time I could hear the hubbub growing louder and louder as I walked back with each ball. It may have been what they came to see but I'd bowled Boycott five of the best balls I could and he was still there. Could I keep it up? Had he ridden out the storm? The roar after the fifth ball was deafening and, as I walked back for the last, I tried to imagine what Boycott would be thinking. I reckoned he'd be expecting another short one on the grounds that I'd been stirred up by the crowd. So I aimed instead for a full length on off stump. Sure enough, he didn't move into line, the ball moved away a little and passed outside his bat by a couple of inches.

The next thing I knew, bedlam had erupted all around the ground. For a split second, I was dazed. Boycott was not a batsman who was bowled very often and I certainly didn't expect I could hit his off stump like that. My view was blocked by his pads so I didn't see the stump cartwheeling out of the ground and only fully realised what had happened when Desmond Haynes rushed over from his position at short-leg to embrace me in congratulations and the slip fielders followed.

I didn't even see Geoff making his way past me back to the pavilion.

As I made my way back to my fielding position on the fine-leg boundary in front of the Three Ws Stand, people were standing and cheering. Some came on to the field to shake my hand, even a few of the hundreds of sun-pink English fans down for the Test on package holidays. Slowly, it dawned on me that I had bowled a quite special over but there wasn't the normal elation I felt at clean bowling a top batsman. More than anything, I was trying to work out how I'd managed to pass Geoff Boycott's usually broad bat on the outside and still hit the off stump. Apparently Geoff was equally baffled. As he later admitted, he was so devastated to be out in that way that he spent several hours reviewing the TV replays to see where he went wrong.

It was one of those days when everything was in my favour and everything clicked. Later in the day, when Clive brought me back for a second spell from the same end, I got right back into the groove from the first ball and dismissed Ian Botham and David Bairstow in my opening over. Over a much longer period, it was similar in the Oval Test against England in 1976, when

4

I took a record 14 wickets for 149 in the match. There were other times when, strive as hard as I could, it was impossible to coordinate pace and control.

These are vagaries of the great game I grew up in Jamaica accepting and appreciating, encouraged by my father and family and by an environment in which cricket was revered and practised with a religious zeal. That over to Geoff Boycott, and those wickets at The Oval, had their origins on the concrete pitch in the backyard of the Holding residence in Dunrobin Avenue and on the playing fields at Redhills Oval, at Jamaica College's Clovelly Park and at the Melbourne Club ground in Kingston, long before I ever dreamt that whatever talent I had would transform me into a bowler capable of such deeds.

CHAPTER 2

From spin to pace

My father, Ralph, has always been a keen sportsman. In his heyday, he was better as a footballer than a cricketer but he played both games for the Melbourne Club, one of the oldest in Jamaica which marked its hundredth year in 1992. He was also very involved in the administration of the club and served for some time as its president.

As a dedicated cricket fan, he seldom missed a major match at Sabina Park and would have been in happy mood as he watched the first Test of the 1954 series between England, led by Len Hutton, and the West Indies, under Jeffrey Stollmeyer. Not only did the West Indies win by 140 runs but his great friend and fellow Melbourne member, Esmond Kentish, took five second-innings wickets to clinch the victory. A few weeks later, there was another event for him to celebrate – or so I should hope! On 16 February 1954 I arrived as the new addition to the Holding family, born at 29 Dunrobin Avenue, Kingston, the fourth child and second son. A few days later, I was christened Michael Anthony.

Ours was always a loving, closely-knit family. Dad was then, and still is, a private building contractor, self-taught and hard-working. Enid, my mother, was a schoolteacher who trained in both Jamaica and England. Rheima and Marjorie were the two girls, born in that order, followed by Ralph junior, with yours truly coming in at no. 11 in the order, so to speak. I suppose Mum's training as a teacher made her a strict disciplinarian and, whenever I strayed from the straight and narrow, she was the one to act as both judge and jury. Dad was the executioner who meted out the appropriate punishment! But such occasions were rare and my boyhood days are filled with memories of a happy family and the outdoor life which the consistently warm Jamaican climate encourages.

We lived near an open gully in the Dunrobin area of the capital, Kingston, ideal ground for the neighbourhood boys to arrange our cricket and football games. The sun seemed to be always shining and our games, or just our boyish skylarking, would stretch from sunrise to sunset. Sometimes, we'd take a brief break for lunch before we were off again.

It's a schedule all West Indian mothers learn to live with but at least mine had the facility to do something about it. I'm sure it was her influence that persuaded Dad to do a little of his construction work in the form of a concrete pitch out back which kept me at home more often and meant Mum's lunch didn't go to waste. By then, I believe she had come to accept that her youngest son's inclinations were more sporting than musical for, while my sisters and brother took to the piano that was always in the house, I could not make head or tail of it. Miss Helps, the music instructor, soon advised the family they were wasting their money sending me to classes.

It was the outdoor life for me and I got plenty of encouragement from Dad who provided me with the approved coaching books to improve my game and tagged me along to all the big matches at Sabina. At that age, sitting in one place for the whole day wasn't my idea of fun. Playing cricket and football with my friends was more my thing, so I would try and miss those trips to Sabina whenever I could. The benefit of watching the stars had to wait while I did my own playing, either at Redhills Oval or at my first school, Peterkin's Preparatory, on Brentford Road.

By the time I was ten, I was ready for my first representative match and there was plenty of excitement around the house when I proudly announced I was in the Dunrobin area team for a Rankine Cup match at Redhills Oval. The Rankine Cup was a competition between community teams but, as far as the Holding household was concerned, it could have been a Test – and Test cricketers need to be properly attired. There was, therefore, a great deal of panic when we realised I needed a pair of long white trousers for the big occasion, a crisis that led to my elder sister hurriedly driving her kid brother to the shops at nearby Tropical Plaza in search of cricket trousers. As it turned out, all we could find were a rather flashy pair, obviously meant for something more formal than a cricket match. But they would have to do and I appeared that day at least well turned out.

I can't remember now how I fared in the game but I fancied myself at the time as something of an off-spinner who could bat a bit. I must have shown some promise since Dad began taking a serious interest in my cricket as I got older. He organised coaching sessions on the concrete pitch at home from Teddy Griffith and also included me whenever he could in the friendly matches he would organise, and captain, for Melbourne, mainly playing against Rankine Cup teams and, every now and again, venturing into the country, to Kirkvine, to play the bauxite company, Alcan.

I may not have recognised it at the time but it was a wonderful grounding for a budding young cricketer. Teddy Griffith was the son of the famous Barbados and West Indies fast bowler of an earlier generation, Herman Griffith, who once bowled Don Bradman for 0 in a Test at Sydney in 1931 when the West Indies won their first Test, though not the series, against Australia. Teddy had emigrated to Jamaica and consistently played for the island as a left-handed opening batsman and right-arm medium-pacer. He worked session after session on the basics, trying to persuade his reluctant young recruit to get his left-arm high on delivery and prodding him to play with bat close to front leg, an exercise which I took so literally that I ended up with several sore toes and insteps. It may explain my eventual modest batting record but the guidance I received from Teddy Griffith when I was twelve and thirteen was invaluable.

It was also an advantage playing in the Melbourne Sunday sides, with Dad as captain, and going down with him to the club to practise in the nets. The club then boasted several players with first-class experience for Jamaica such as Bruce Wellington, an excellent left-arm spinner who always had time to give words of advice and encouragement, and Arthur Barrett, a leg-spinner who went on to play Test cricket. Sam Morgan, a solid opener, was another Jamaica player at Melbourne at the time. And, of course, there was still Teddy Griffith.

In fact, I kept on turning out for Melbourne even after I started my secondary education at Kingston College in 1965, aged eleven. It was only after the games master, Trevor Parchment, learned I was playing club cricket that I was drafted into the College team at junior colts, or under-fourteen, level.

I thoroughly enjoyed my schooldays. I was following in the footsteps of my father and brother, who had both been educated at KC, and soon after I enrolled, one of my sisters joined the staff to be followed by my mother, who had previously been the Principal of St George's Primary School. It was a family connection that bound us closer to one of Jamaica's most illustrious boys' schools. Among the main secondary schools in Kingston there is a strong sporting tradition, the rivalry is keen, competition fierce and standards high, as you would expect of an island that has produced not only great cricketers but great athletes as well. I thrived in such an environment. If it wasn't cricket, I'd be playing soccer or training with the track and field team for the big annual inter-schools championships that have always filled the National Stadium to its 25,000-capacity. The stars of the meet could expect to be spotted by talent scouts who flew in from the United States for the occasion to offer athletic scholarships on behalf of their universities.

Not that I ever aspired to those heights. My soccer was only moderate and, after I made my name in the cricket team, Trevor Parchment put an end to my playing it. I might be injured, he said, I wasn't going to be another Pelé and it just wasn't worth it. I do have some little claim to fame in athletics as I still hold the high jump record for the under-12 class at KC – all of 4 feet, 11¼ inches. I also did the hurdles, but the story which went the rounds when I first made it into the West Indies team, that I was a potential 400-metres Olympic champion, was a case of mistaken identity. I did open the bowling in the Jamaica youth team with Seymour Newman who had speed both as a bowler and a runner. He chose the latter course, duly took up his track and field scholarship in America and developed into the world record-holder at 800 metres and a finalist in the 1976 Olympics.

I stuck to cricket because it was the sport I enjoyed most, perhaps because it was also the best organised. From the time a schoolboy goes into his junior colts team in Jamaica and shows some talent, his progression through the system is well planned, and so it was in my case. My first captain at KC was Sydney Headley, youngest son of the great George, the cricketing legend whose popularity has never been surpassed by any other sportsman in Jamaica. Sydney, as I remember him, was a very talented batsman himself but he wasn't committed to the game and eventually left Jamaica to live in Africa. All round us, in pictures on the walls and in the talk from our elders, were reminders of the school's great deeds and outstanding players, such as J.K. Holt and Easton McMorris, both Test batsmen. Our arch-rivals in the Sunlight Cup were Wolmer's, which boasted several West Indies Test cricketers among its old boys, including two captains, Karl Nunes and Gerry Alexander. Their side at the time included Philip Rae, son of another of Wolmer's Test men, Allan Rae, and a mere stripling of a lad who was engulfed by his pads. His name was Jeffrey Dujon.

Most of Jamaica's cricketers have developed through the schools system and there is great tradition, and rivalry, between them: Kingston College (KC), Wolmer's, Jamaica College (JC), Calabar, St George's and the newer ones such as Excelsior (XLCR). They all have strong alumni and those who have made it in sports or politics, or any other field, are feted as heroes.

By the time I got to KC, I had changed from off-spinner to fast bowler, what they call in Jamaica 'a pacer in a hurry'. It was a switch prompted by our games at Redhills Oval. The rules were simple. It was every man for himself. If you got the ball, you bowled and if you got the batsman out, you batted. The drawback was that you had to hit the stumps since whoever took your catch would qualify as next in and there was no leg-before-wicket. So the only way to make batsmen without pads get their legs out of the way of the cork and tar ball was to bowl as fast as you could. Otherwise, they would just grin and bear it and keep on batting. I soon learned the benefits of switching from spin to pace.

I had already developed my long run-up. I would use it almost throughout my career for no more profound reason than that I felt most comfortable with it and found I could bowl a good outswinger although I didn't generate much pace. When I first came into the KC senior team, our captain was Zeph Henry who relied on his namesake, Norman Henry, decidedly quick, and Raymond Forde, left-arm swing, as his main attack. I was the fifth bowler and hardly got a chance until, eventually, Zeph turned to me in one match as a last resort to dislodge a troublesome pair. I got a wicket in my first over and four in the innings and my credentials were established.

In my final year at school I led the KC team to the Sunlight Cup with an unbeaten record. We were not bowled out once, yet bowled the opposition out each time, and finished with 37 out of a maximum 39 points. My own return was 40 wickets at an average of less than four runs a wicket. I was more pleased with the way we played together as a team and by a comment by Baz Freckleton, a sports columnist in the *Daily Gleaner* newspaper, who wrote: 'Throughout the season, the champions displayed an admirable blend of cricket skills, discipline, sportsmanship and sensitivity to good manners'.

By this time, I had already moved up the ladder, into the Jamaica under-19 team, for the annual West Indies youth championships and, in 1973, into the Jamaica team proper for the regional Shell Shield tournament. When I was first picked for the youth team in 1971, I was as well prepared as I could be. My father had provided me with all the support any boy could ask for and Jimmy Richards, an old boy of the school who took over as KC coach in 1971, was an inspiration. Jimmy was more than just a coach. He was like a father to the boys, involved in our day-to-day living, advising us as much about life itself as cricket, making sure he turned out not only cricketers but well-rounded individuals. Often, he would even pay school fees himself or buy gear for boys he felt couldn't afford it.

He lived for cricket and for KC, and I owe him a debt of gratitude for the early training I received from him. He is still very much associated with the game as one of the Caribbean's leading statisticians and commentators.

As training for that 1971 tournament, held in Jamaica, the squad spent a month at the army camp in Kingston under the tutelage of J. K. Holt and Alf Valentine, who were both government coaches, and we were rewarded for our preparation by winning the championship for the first time. I only took seven wickets in our three matches and was somewhat overshadowed by Seymour Newman who collected a dozen. Jamaica gave up the title in Barbados the next year, when the combined Windward and Leeward Islands won on their first year of entry.

The youth tournament is the first experience for the young West Indian cricketer of what concentrated, top-class competition is like. It is organised along the same lines as the senior Red Stripe Cup in that all the territories play against each other except that the teams congregate in one island where the tournament is held. In my three years it proved a great, if tough assignment, with four three-day matches packed into the space of two-and-a-half weeks.

I believe there is no similar competition at that age

level anywhere else in the world, and it has stood the West Indies in good stead. Among those I played with or against in those three seasons were Larry Gomes, Faoud Bacchus, Jeffrey Dujon, Joel Garner and Colin Croft, with all of whom I would later play Test cricket. The first time I came across 'Crofty', who was to cause so much discomfort to Test batsmen a few years on with his pace and awkwardly angled deliveries, was in 1971 in Jamaica. When they told us that this big, strapping man was Guyana's fast bowler, I could see our batsmen quaking in their boots. He certainly didn't look an ordinary nineteen-year-old but we were lucky that we met him on a slow pitch and he didn't cause any damage.

The youth tournaments only started in the 1960s and they have been supplemented by regular under-19 series against England and, more recently, Australia, all of which has given an important new dimension to the development of our cricketers. Cynics point out that Headley, Sobers, the three Ws – Worrell, Weekes and Walcott – Ramadhin, Valentine and other great West Indians of the past came through without such exposure but they were all exceptional cricketers, the type who would come through in any circumstances. Now the net is spread wider and even the moderate players are well prepared when they come into the first-class game.

Like most sportsmen, I faced the dilemma of how to balance school work and play. Taking on as much cricket as I was, my studies inevitably suffered. As it was, I gained five O-level passes and then went on to spend two years in KC's sixth form, aiming for A-levels. For much of these last two years I concentrated on cricket. Appreciating the possibilities of my going further in the game, my father and my headmaster, Douglas Forrest, were proud of my achievements on the field. So was my mother, but she kept reminding me that cricket is not forever. At the time, though, it was not a serious career option.

CHAPTER 3

Moving into the real world

I made my debut for Jamaica in the Shell Shield against Barbados at Sabina Park in 1973. I was a month short of my nineteenth birthday and in my last year at school. I had a couple of seasons in the annual youth championships and was in the Melbourne first team in the Senior Cup competition, so I was ready for the promotion. Throughout the West Indies the standard of club cricket is not that much short of first-class level, although it has been seriously affected lately by the loss of so many of our players to the English counties and leagues for at least part of the year.

In the early 1970s very few Jamaicans had those opportunities, and all the top clubs included several Jamaican representatives and even a few with Test caps. At Melbourne, we had Arthur Barrett, the leg-spinner who had played against India and England, as well as Sam Morgan, an opening bat, Cecil Lawson, a tall, left-arm fast bowler, and Bruce Wellington, a left-arm spinner, all with good Shell Shield records. Kensington could boast eight or nine first-class players including Lawrence Rowe, Uton Dowe and the wicketkeeper, Desmond Lewis, all Test men, while other Test caps were Easton McMorris at Lucas and Maurice Foster at Kingston. Each of the clubs had a strong following and big crowds would turn out for the key matches which were spread over two Saturdays.

16

More recently, Jamaica has followed most of the other territories by extending the matches to three days so that batsmen have even more time to build an innings and bowlers have meaningful spells. Prior to the Shell Shield – or, as it is now, the Red Stripe Cup – trials involving the leading players are held so that no-one should find the step up the ladder into the Jamaican team too overwhelming.

But a shock awaited me when I turned up at Sabina Park for my first Shield match. Although I was young, considered myself fit and trained and practised regularly, I was astonished to see Uton Dowe, then the fastest bowler in the West Indies and the spearhead of the Jamaican attack, jogging two or three laps around the outfield before the start of play. He returned to the dressing-room, sweating profusely, only to start skipping. To me that seemed sheer madness. Surely all this exertion would leave him exhausted after bowling a couple of overs in the heat in the middle?

In those days, none of the teams went through any serious training or had a trainer. You just put on your whites, went out half an hour or so prior to play and had a little knock-up on the outfield. It was only much later, when the tough Australian, Dennis Waight, was assigned to the West Indies squad in World Series Cricket, that I appreciated what fitness was all about – and realised that Dowe had really only been warming up.

So it was that, on my first day at Sabina Park against Barbados, Dowe ran up and bowled fast, over after over, while his new, young partner found himself puffing and panting after four overs, leaning on the fence in front of the bleachers at third man, head hung down, hoping that skipper Maurice Foster wouldn't call on me again. I had run in with all the enthusiasm of a first-timer desperate to prove something, telling myself this was the real thing and that I had to bowl flat out. No line and length stuff here, everyone was expecting me to be quick. Perhaps I tried too hard and blew myself out too quickly. Perhaps it was nervous exhaustion. But I doubt it. I just was not fit enough, not prepared enough.

Fortunately the powers-that-be seemed more impressed with what everyone kept referring to as my 'potential' and the fact that, in Jamaica's match against the touring Australians at Sabina a few weeks later, I twice clean bowled the opening batsman, Ian Redpath, for 14 and 1. They were my only two wickets and that was only my third first-class match. So I was surprised when I was included in the President's XI, a sort of West Indies second eleven, to play against the Australians at Jarrett Park in Montego Bay the following week. It was looked on as a trial for our up-and-coming players but most of us were too young and inexperienced to make any show in that company. We lost badly, but it is interesting to note that Clive Lloyd was captain, the first time he had been appointed to the post at any level by the West Indies selectors, and that Gordon Greenidge and Viv Richards were both on a representative team for the first time. I only managed a single wicket in the match but it happened to be Redpath again, bowled for 0. It was the kind of sequence that gets the fans and the newspapers going and I probably got more notice for that than if I'd taken three or four wickets in the match.

By the August of that year, it was time to leave school, where I had spent so many happy years, and search for a job in the real world. Neither my parents nor I had thought seriously of cricket as a full-time career since, at the time, even those at the top were paid very little and it lacked any type of security. So what then? I was always good with figures and was in the science stream at Kingston College where mathematics was my strongest subject. It followed, I suppose, that I would apply to a bank. I wrote to Barclays, was almost immediately accepted and, as the bank was just beginning to get computerised, was assigned to its new computer centre, an exciting prospect.

I was never really worried about the job possibly clashing with my cricket because employers in the West Indies are usually quite liberal when it comes to giving time off to cricketers. The territorial teams, certainly back then although to a lesser extent now, comprised mainly amateurs who held down jobs outside the game and who had to rely on their bosses to release them to play. I had never heard of any player having a problem and didn't anticipate one myself until I applied for time to play for Jamaica in the 1974 Shell Shield. I was told I could have it but as no-pay leave. That might have been fair enough but, when the season was over, the manager called me into his office, threw some questions about how I saw my future in cricket and advised that he doubted whether the bank could accommodate my absences in future.

As soon as I got home that evening, I sat down and wrote my letter of resignation. It was probably the rash decision of impulsive youth for I had no other job to go to and cricket certainly couldn't make me a living. But I loved the game and wasn't prepared to let anything spoil it.

Something, I felt, would come along before very long, and so it did. Michael Manley, who was then the Prime Minister, is as avid a cricket fan as I have ever known and when he came to hear I wasn't working, he arranged an interview for me with the government's computer department which I joined in 1974. Since the government had a regulation that made leave mandatory for any of its employees chosen as national sporting representatives, it was a very acceptable arrangement.

At the time, I had no realistic prospects as a full-time professional cricketer. I saw my long-term future very much in computer-programming and, in 1976, took up a government scholarship for a four-year course in computer science at the University of the West Indies (UWI), preparing for a life in the civil service. But within a year, an Australian businessman by the name of Kerry Packer made his revolutionary entrance into international cricket and his World Series Cricket changed my life.

Had it not been for that development, I would probably have been forced to give up Test cricket to pursue the course at the UWI and guarantee my future, although I cannot envisage myself ever sitting at a desk doing an eight-to-four job. As it was, I officially remained employed with the government's computer department until 1981 where everyone, not least my boss, Laurice Abrahams, was always friendly and understanding. I think they basked a little in the glory of the success of the West Indies team but, when I signed up to play Lancashire League cricket for Rishton in 1981, my conscience finally got the better of me and I felt I should resign. But I still occasionally wonder what might have been.

As it was, my early selection to play for the President's XI against the 1973 Australians was a hint that a place in the full West Indies team might not be far away even though I knew, within myself, that I was still somewhere short of that level.

I lost almost all the following 1974 Shell Shield season, being confined to the physiotherapist's table with a pulled groin muscle after bowling only seven overs for the President's XI in Barbados, the opening match against that year's touring team, England. It was the first of the many injuries which were to follow me throughout my career but, aged twenty and bursting with enthusiasm, I felt this one most, in every sense. It was no fun sitting in the pavilion, knowing my season was over, while the other aspiring bowlers struggled in the middle as Geoff Boycott prepared for the series ahead with an unbeaten 262 in an England total of 511 for four declared.

CHAPTER 4

Learning the hard way

By the time the 1974 Jamaica club season started, my leg had mended and, a little older, bigger and stronger, I noticed a definite increase in my pace. I have never been physically big and strong like so many of our great West Indian fast bowlers – 'naturally wiry' was how one schoolmaster described me – and I owed my development to the weight training that 'Youngster' Goldsmith put me through in my later days at KC. A hard taskmaster, Goldsmith was mainly responsible for preparing the track and field and soccer teams but he also recognised that, as a budding fast bowler, I needed some more body and stamina.

In 1974 I took all ten wickets in an innings against Boys' Town in the Senior Cup competition and, even in the presence of Uton Dowe and Junior Williams, two far more experienced bowlers, I was given first use of the new ball for Jamaica in the 1975 Shell Shield.

I now had the self-confidence every cricketer needs, charging in to bowl rather than just trotting in, and produced a spell against Guyana in Georgetown that was to prove very significant.

A year earlier, in our Shell Shield match against Guyana at Sabina Park, I had toiled for 24 overs to finish with no wicket for 107 as Clive Lloyd and Alvin Kallicharran added 241 for the fifth wicket, Lloyd 134, Kallicharran 197. I was sure I had Lloyd lbw when I hit him three times on the pads in one over and, even if umpire Paynter didn't agree, I could tell Lloyd was impressed with my advance since he had captained me for the President's XI against the Australians the season before. By the time we met again, in the 1975 Shell Shield, Lloyd had been appointed West Indies captain in succession to Rohan Kanhai and had just returned from his first overseas series, in India, which the West Indies won 3–2. The pitch at Bourda in Georgetown has always been a fast bowler's nightmare, easy-paced and with no bounce, and Guyana's batting was intimidating. The first four in the order, Roy Fredericks, Len Baichan, Kallicharran and Lloyd, all left-handers, were in the West Indies team on the tour of India, so I knew that, when I dismissed Fredericks for 8 and Kallicharran for 0 in my opening spell, I had achieved something. One of Lloyd's trump cards in India had been a new, young fast bowler by the name of Andy Roberts, who broke a West Indies record with 32 wickets in the series, and I sensed that Lloyd was keen to have me in his West Indies team as a partner for Roberts.

I developed an immediate admiration for Clive Lloyd from the time I first played under him against the Australians at Montego Bay in 1973. He had an obvious interest in all of his players and a quiet, approachable manner. He was a caring captain, one you felt like playing for. It was an assessment that I never had cause to change.

The next West Indies assignment after the 1975 home season was the first World Cup in England. I was then twenty-one and might have made the team except that the selectors were not inclined to subject a raw fast bowler to the peculiar conditions of one-day cricket on his debut, as J. K. Holt, who was then on the panel, reported to friends of mine.

23

When, later in the year, I was picked for the tour of Australia, it did not come as much of a surprise to me as it must have done to most people. After all, at that point, I had only played a handful of first-class matches over three seasons and had taken only sixteen wickets. The team was announced during a club match at Melbourne and my first reaction when I heard it was that it would be my first time away from home for any length of time – three-and-a-half months away from Jamaica.

By the end of it, I was telling my father, who travelled through Australia specially to follow the tour, that if that was what West Indies cricket was about, I wanted no part of it. We were badly beaten 5–1 in the six-Test series, but it was more than the pain of defeat that left me disillusioned. I was shocked and appalled by the attitude and behaviour of some of our players, astonished by the abominable, biased umpiring, and upset by the way we generally played in Australia.

It was probably because we were going through such a bad time that some people just lost their cool. At team meetings, certain players would show no respect to the captain, Lloyd, or to the manager, Esmond Kentish, the former Jamaica fast bowler who was my father's friend, while relationships between some individuals reached boiling point and, in some instances, boiled over.

As a prep-form boy in my first term, so to speak, I did not feel it was my place to intervene but there was one occasion when I could not restrain myself. After a particularly heated exchange at the Windsor Hotel in Melbourne, Alvin Kallicharran, a senior player, exploded in anger after he and Keith Boyce got into some argument over the hook shot that cost us so many wickets in the series. Kallicharran let everyone have a piece of his mind and stormed out of the team meeting without asking leave of captain or manager. I chased after him and tried to persuade him to come back to sort things out but it proved futile.

There was plenty of other argument and dissent at meetings and in the dressing-room, and things did not improve any when Lloyd told the press after the match that we might well have won the fourth Test in Sydney had not Keith Boyce dropped Greg Chappell when he was 11 out of his eventual 182 not out. The reporter put it the other way round, that Boyce's miss caused us to lose. There is a subtle difference and it caused another big stink in the camp.

We were on edge mainly because we did not feel we were being given a fair crack of the whip by the umpiring. No West Indies team had ever won a series in Australia and we came with high hopes of reversing that, following our two victories over the Aussies in the World Cup in England the previous summer, including the final. We weren't underestimating them by any means and knew full well how, a year earlier, they had demolished England with their feared fast attack of Dennis Lillee and Jeff Thomson. Yet we had fire-power of our own and strong batting. We were sure of our prospects.

Australia won the first Test at Brisbane by eight wickets although the result was closer than the margin shows. We then drew level with an innings-victory at Perth where Roy Fredericks made his phenomenal 169 in 212 minutes with 27 fours and a six, and Andy Roberts took seven for 54 in the second innings. After that, it was all downhill and, while no-one can dispute that Australia fielded a powerful team, nothing will ever convince me they were not helped by the umpiring. There were too many clear-cut decisions that went against us to call them genuine errors while, throughout the series, our non-striking batsmen could clearly see Lillee and Thomson overstepping the front crease without being called for no-ball. Well before the end, our spirit was broken and we were divided among ourselves. There is no way you can wage a campaign like that, in cricket or in anything else, and we were trounced.

The most celebrated, and crucial, incident of the series occurred in the fourth Test at Sydney and involved me personally. We were 2–1 down and struggling to get back on even terms. We batted consistently to score 355 in our first innings, a good start. Australia began solidly but lost two wickets just before tea on the second day and, with my first ball after the interval, I had Ian Redpath caught behind to make it 103 for three.

In came Ian Chappell, the Australian scalp we always wanted to get more than any other. I will always remember the first ball I bowled him. Trying for an inswinger, I deliverd it from wide of the crease but, as sometimes happens, it moved away on pitching. He drove at it, got an outside edge and the ball went straight into wicketkeeper Deryck Murray's gloves. There was jubilation in the unanimous appeal for, with two wickets from two balls right after tea and Australia 103 for four, we were back on top. Then I realised the umpire, Reg Ledwidge, had given it not out. I just could not believe it. It was too obvious but, when I looked back at him in appeal, he had a strange smile on his face and was shaking his head. At the other end, Chappell had his head down, marking his crease with his boot-tip and adjusting his box in the self-conscious manner of a child caught with his hand in the cookie jar.

I had never come across anything like it, not in any kind of cricket. And this was supposed to be Test cricket, the highest grade that there is. We were already suspicious of the umpiring after our experiences in the previous Test in Melbourne during which Lloyd openly criticised the decisions, especially of one official, Jack Collins. Lance Gibbs was driven to exasperation and drew a lot of flak from the press for refusing to hand Collins his sun hat, preferring to bowl with it stuck in the back of his trousers as a mark of protest. Injury kept me out of that match so I didn't encounter that umpiring first-hand, but it hit me forcibly in Sydney. It was just too much to take and I found myself, uncontrollable and inconsolable, weeping tears of frustration by the side of the pitch, looking up at Lance Gibbs, who had rushed over from gully to comfort me. All I could say to him was: 'I'm not bowling another ball. I done!'

The ironic twist to the story was that Lance, a veteran of two previous Australian tours in 1960–61 and 1968–69, had warned us what to expect of the umpiring and pleaded with us not to let it get us down as it would affect our cricket. And it was Lance who was the first to lose his cool at the decisions of umpire Collins in Melbourne. Now, however, I appreciated his quick attention.

After what seemed an eternity, and with tears still in my eyes, I did bowl again and, a little later, got umpire Ledwidge to raise his finger for another big edge by Chappell to Murray after he had made 4. But if Lance hadn't come across, put his arm around my shoulders and talked quietly and logically about getting on with the game, I have often wondered what might have been.

The fact was that I simply could not come to terms with what was going on. The ideals I had been brought up on about the umpires' impartiality were shattered on my first international tour. A few years later, Chappell called it his most embarrassing moment in cricket but he emphasised that he never 'walked'. That certainly was no consolation to me and there would be times in the future, notably in New Zealand in 1980, when similar injustices occurred and I reacted in similar fashion but without Gibbs to calm me down.

At the age of twenty-one, with so little top-class cricket behind me, I expected to be no more than a reserve, there mainly to learn. Whatever else went on, however, I immediately took to Australia as a country, with its high standard of living, its sporting people and its superb cricket grounds, and this translated into a couple of good performances in the early state matches. I felt relaxed in my run-up and delivery and was able to generate real pace, especially when I had what were then my best figures of six for 60 to bowl us to victory over New South Wales at Sydney. What is more, I was hitting the ball so unusually well that I made 51 not out against South Australia and 62 against New South Wales. These were my first half-centuries in any standard of cricket and were every bit as satisfying as the wickets. For all that, I didn't have any visions of a place in the Test team since Roberts, Vanburn Holder, Boyce and Bernard Julien were all well established. It was only when Deryck Murray, the vice-captain, came to me at practice in Brisbane that I had any hint. He told me I wouldn't be playing in the state match against Queensland since I might be wanted for the Test the following week in which case I would have to be fresh. I suspect it was an early warning to get mentally prepared as well, although there was no way I could have anticipated what actually happened.

I was flattered, first of all, to find myself batting at no. 8 in the order but then flabbergasted to be going in to bat half an hour before lunch on my first day in Test cricket. Lloyd won the toss, we batted and the board on the hill at the 'Gabba read 99 for six when I came in to join Deryck Murray. Lillee, Thomson and Gary

Gilmour were straining at the leash and there seemed to be a hundred Australians all around me. But I managed to hang around for some time to add 72 with Deryck, scoring 34 in a total of 214. It was cause for immediate promotion to no. 3 in the second innings but that was only temporary, as night-watchman after Gordon Greenidge was out for his second 0 late on the third afternoon.

As I quickly found out, if I was going to pretend to be a batsman, I had to expect to be treated like one and I took blows on the elbow from Thomson in the first innings and on the chest from Gilmour in the second. I ended the match with an enhanced, but rather misleading, reputation as a batsman, a few bruises and not a single wicket.

At Perth, I went through most of the opening day still searching for that elusive first Test wicket before Andy Roberts, with whom I had already struck up what was to be a close and lasting friendship, came up with some helpful advice. The pitch at the WACA in those days was easily the fastest I had ever bowled on but I still hadn't taken a wicket late in the afternoon when Andy came across and suggested I try to give Max Walker a rising ball, short of a length around the off stump, and he would push it into the slips. I was dog-tired at the time and let Andy know as much but he insisted. Somehow, I found just enough strength to bang one in, Walker fended it off and I was the happiest and certainly the most relieved man on the field when I saw Richards hold the catch at third slip.

Lloyd had consoled me prior to the match, when I must have been looking a little sorry for myself, by assuring me the wickets would come before long. Next morning, I got three more very quickly with the second new ball – Ian Chappell, who made 156, Jeff Thomson first ball, and finally Ashley Mallett, all bowled. We played our best cricket in that Test as the result revealed, victory by an innings and 87 runs with a day to spare after Fredericks' blazing century, Lloyd's 149 and Andy Roberts' seven wickets in the second innings.

Unfortunately, everything went downhill after that for me personally and for the team. I strained a groin muscle midway through Australia's second innings in the Perth Test, had to miss the third in Melbourne, and then ended the tour limping off the Melbourne Cricket Ground on the second day of the last Test when my groin muscle went again while I was fielding. The outcome was a crushing disappointment since so much had been expected of the team, but it taught us some important lessons and forcibly brought home to me just how tough international cricket was.

Clive Lloyd was comparatively new to the captaincy and both he and manager Kentish were far too soft in dealing with those players who challenged their authority and whose negative attitudes only increased our problems on the field. I'm sure Clive realised this afterwards, for he was soon to become a firm and outstanding leader.

He took careful note, too, of the telling effect of genuine fast bowling. We had heard plenty of Lillee and Thomson but we were confident we had the batsmen to deal with them. Perhaps we were lulled into a false sense of security by the way Lloyd, Kallicharran and Fredericks, especially, had treated them in the World Cup only a few months before. In Australian conditions, they proved to be something else.

'Thommo' was the one who really made the difference. Everyone knew Lillee was a class bowler who could get you out with more than just pace although he was fast enough. But his partner presented the additional fear of physical danger. I still haven't seen anyone bowl quicker than he did in that series. With his obvious strength and his slinging action, like a whiplash, he had the ability to bowl the unplayable ball. When Lawrence Rowe got an especially nasty bouncer in Adelaide that took his glove and went to first slip, he came back to the dressing-room and announced: 'Not even God could play that!'

Lillee was the complete fast bowler, with a magnificent action and superb control and variation, and they made a perfect combination. I understand it was the same with Wes Hall and Charlie Griffith for the West Indies in the 1960s, Hall the equivalent of Lillee, Griffith a West Indian Thomson. Thomson had nothing like Lillee's control and would sprinkle wides, full tosses and half volleys among his better deliveries. But when you've got extreme pace, you can get away with the bad ball and the good one is often going to pick up a wicket. With such an unorthodox action, I wasn't surprised Thomson did not last much longer than ten years. But in that series, he was an awesome proposition, his influence even greater than his tally of 29 wickets suggests.

These were the days before helmets, arm-guards and chest protectors and several of our batsmen were hit. The most serious injuries were Kallicharran's broken nose in Perth and Julien's broken thumb in Sydney when someone had the bright idea of making him open the batting for the first time in his life after Greenidge failed. Thomson always seemed to be on everyone's mind – not Lillee, nor the Chappell brothers or Ian Redpath who all made heaps of runs. Thomson and, of course, the umpiring.

We should have had the ammunition to reply in kind but our fast bowlers were seldom fit together. Roberts bowled magnificently, at Perth especially, but he had to carry most of the load and broke down in the fifth Test. Keith Boyce strained his back, Bernard Julien was ruled out for the last two Tests by his cracked thumb and my groin muscle kept me out of the third and sixth Tests. So yet another West Indies team came back from Australia with its tail between its legs. But the disappointment of the captain and the players was accompanied by a silent determination that such a disaster would not be allowed to happen again.

CHAPTER 5

In rhythm at The Oval

There is an old and proven theory that, if you fall off a horse, jump straight back on again or, out of fear, you might never ride again. Having got back from Australia in early February 1976 it was undoubtedly best for us that we went straight into a Test series at home, even if our opponents this time happened to be a somewhat calmer creature than the bucking bronco that had thrown us to the ground in Australia.

The Indians were our visitors and, as Deryck Murray commented at the time, our batsmen all had to learn to play forward again. In Australia, they had been forced on to the back foot by Thomson, Lillee and the others, but the Indians had no-one above medium-pace and we had to contend, instead, with a quartet of the game's finest spinners, Bishan Bedi, Chandrasekhar, Venkataraghavan and Erapally Prasanna.

It proved a close, hard-fought series as India also boasted very strong batting with Sunil Gavaskar, Gundappa Viswanath, Mohinder Amarnath and Brijesh Patel as their main run-getters. We had to win the final Test at Sabina Park to clinch it 2–1.

Beyond the result, the series carried considerable long-term significance. It marked the end of the career of Lance Gibbs, the last of the great West Indian spinners who, in the final Test at Melbourne, had surpassed Freddie Trueman's wicket-taking Test record of 307. Lance was then aged forty-one, still fit and competitive, but he was not summoned against India. Even if he felt he still deserved his place on merit, the selectors decided they would search for a replacement against the Indians. Captain Lloyd and vice-captain Murray, on the other hand, were coming round to the view that it was pointless having a spinner simply for so-called balance and that, in future, the West Indies should completely rely on our strength, namely pace.

The philosophy had begun to take root in Australia and gained ground following the two Tests against India at the Queen's Park Oval when those aspiring to fill Gibbs' boots – the left-handed Raphick Jumadeen, the off-spinner Albert Padmore and the leg-spinners David Holford and Imtiaz Ali – failed to make an impression on the one spinners' pitch in the Caribbean. India scored 402 for five declared in the first of the Queen's Park Tests and, when rain caused the Georgetown Test to be switched to Queen's Park as well, they created history by amassing 406 for four to win the match after Lloyd had declared to give his bowlers time to effect victory.

After that match, Clive never depended on spin again. Whatever its origins, the application of the pure pace policy was to change the face of West Indies' and international cricket. Certainly, by the final Test, we had four fast bowlers in the eleven, young Wayne Daniel making his Test debut alongside Vanburn Holder, Bernard Julien and myself even as Andy Roberts was being given a well-deserved rest by the selectors in preparation for the tour of England. In that series, it became standard operating procedure to have four quick bowlers.

India was only my second series but, with Roberts rested, I found myself spearheading the attack and became embroiled in more controversy in the final Test, my first at home at Sabina Park.

As has so often been the case there, the pitch was unpredictable in bounce. Some people claimed there was a ridge but I never detected one. However, several balls were taking off from just short of a length and the Indians did well, after being sent in, to pass 200 for the loss of only one wicket. On that surface, it was inevitable that some batsmen would be hit against such a pace-based attack as ours, especially as we adopted the tactic of bowling from around the wicket, aiming the ball at their bodies. I was not too keen on this method since it gives the batsman little chance of avoiding a bouncer, especially against bowlers with plenty of speed, but it was 1–1 in the series and, after Australia, we were under extreme public pressure to win. Gaekwad, Patel and Viswanath were all hit and injured in India's first innings and Bedi, the Indian captain, declared with six wickets down, calling it 'war' and refusing to bat himself or to send in Chandrasekhar. In the second innings, India batted five men short, were all out for 97 and just barely avoided an innings defeat. It was a bizarre outcome to the match and the series, but not the last time that our fast bowling would stir emotions.

I finished the four Tests against India with 19 wickets at just under 20 runs each and was bubbling with expectation for the tour of England that followed immediately in the summer of 1976. I had never been to England although I had heard a lot about it, mostly from fellow West Indian players who played county and league cricket, and from my mother who studied there as a teacher.

It turned out to be the driest, hottest summer of the century and a highly successful one for the West Indies. Viv Richards rounded off the tour in Australia in a blaze of glory, followed it up with a phenomenal series against India (556 runs in six innings with three centuries) and now reached new heights of brilliance with double-centuries in the first Test at Trent Bridge and the last at The Oval. His 829 runs in the four Tests he played in just passed the West Indies record for a single series held by Clyde Walcott, who happened to be our tour manager. Gordon Greenidge, who failed in Australia and was not picked against India, thrived in conditions in which he had learned most of his cricket with his county, Hampshire. He scored a century in each innings at Old Trafford and both he and his durable partner, the left-handed Roy Fredericks, piled up over 500 runs in the series. The pace policy worked with Roberts and myself sharing 56 wickets, supported by Daniel, Holder and Julien, and the leadership of Lloyd and manager Walcott was confident and assertive, a noticeable contrast to what obtained in Australia. The umpiring, as always in England, was good and could be trusted, and there was no bickering in the team.

Such beneficial changes were reflected in the overall result. After the first two Tests were drawn, we won the last three comfortably to retain the Wisden Trophy and regain our status in world cricket. Yet, for the first month or so, I was hardly involved. Initially, I was bothered by the fact that I was slipping and sliding with my left foot on the delivery stride since I had only brought along the boots that I had used in the West Indies and Australia. These were fine for hard, dry surfaces but, as I discovered, simply didn't grip on the grassier pitches in England. Andy Roberts fixed me up with boots with longer studs but they took some getting used to. Happily, as the heat of the summer took its toll, I found I could revert to my original ones without difficulty.

No sooner had I sorted that out and enjoyed a good performance against a strong MCC side at Lord's, than I was diagnosed as having glandular fever and told I was unlikely to recover in time to play again on tour. My neck and jaw became badly swollen, I found it difficult to eat and, in the nursing home where I was confined, I felt too weak even to get up to turn off the TV set. The whole episode left me feeling quite depressed but, fortunately, the seriousness of my condition had been exaggerated (it was either a bad case of mumps or a mild case of glandular fever) and, although I had to miss the first Test, I was back out in time for the second one at Lord's.

I hardly expected to play since I hadn't had a match for three weeks, but the captain was keen that I should be in the side. I was duly included after a rather inconclusive fitness test on the morning of the match but I was still well short of full fitness. My hopes that we would bat first to give me a little more time to recover were dashed when Clive lost the toss but I still managed to get through nearly fifty overs in the drawn match.

By the time the final Test at The Oval came around, my mystery illness was completely behind me and I proceeded to produce what remained my best performance in any cricket – eight for 92 in the first innings, six for 57 in the second, fourteen for 149 in the match. It was a match in which everything went right for me. With the benefit of hindsight, I believe my youth and enthusiasm were as responsible for the return as anything else. It was a very docile pitch as the scores indicate – West Indies 687 for eight declared and 182 without loss; England 435 and 203. Richards batted as he did for the entire summer for his 291, looking certain to get a triple century before he was bowled by Tony Greig, and Dennis Amiss got a double-century, 203, on his return to the England team.

The more experienced fast bowlers quickly sized things up and decided it was pointless killing themselves in such unhelpful conditions, opting for accurate line and length instead. I was twenty-two years old, fit and young, and I hadn't yet developed the realistic, more cynical, approach that comes with age. I just kept on charging in off my full run and bowling as fast as I could. My rhythm was right, I was accurate, and I kept picking up wickets, but I do feel that the matter-of-fact attitude of the more seasoned fast bowlers helped me to impose myself on proceedings. There were times in later years when I knew I bowled faster although only in short spells and never over such a sustained period as I did at The Oval in that match. For 33 overs in the first innings and another 20.4 in the second, I cannot remember once slackening my pace or even thinking that I should.

There is nothing that thrills a fast bowler more than seeing the stumps flying from behind a batsman and at The Oval I hit them nine times. Not only to my own delight but to the unrestrained delight of every West Indian on the ground as well, I clean bowled Tony Greig in both innings.

Greig had raised our hackles prior to the series by saying, in a television interview, that he would make us 'grovel'. It was his second series as England's captain and we recognised him as a talented, fiercely competitive cricketer from his exploits in the West Indies in 1974 when he was England's outstanding all-rounder. But he was a white South African, qualified to play for England only through his parentage, and 'grovel' was a particularly offensive and ill-chosen word for him to have used in reference to a predominantly black team. It smacked of racism and apartheid and provided us with a very powerful psychological stimulus.

From then on, Greig became a special target and every time he came to the wicket, the fast bowlers seemed to add a yard of pace. His habit of lifting the bat off the ground in his stance made him vulnerable to a yorker, and in the series he was clean bowled five times. Only at Headingley, where he scored 116 and 76 not out with a powerful counter-attack, did he make any runs to speak of. He was nothing if not a showman and, when it was clear we had won the series during our second innings at The Oval, he went down on his hands and knees and himself grovelled. He always had a keen sense of how to get the crowds on his side but his bravado and choice of phrase not only made him a marked man as far as we were concerned but was the starting-point for what became our accepted policy to pay special attention to opposing captains. The theory was, once the head goes, the body must wither. Several batsmen in the England team that summer told me later they hated batting with Greig precisely because the fast bowlers added that extra pace whenever he was in. The subsequent record confirms how many opposing captains were fired, or resigned, after they and/or their teams had failed against the West Indies – Ian Botham and David Gower of England, Kim Hughes of Australia, Geoff Howarth of New Zealand, Kapil Dev and Dilip Vengsarkar of India.

The critical match in 1976 was the third at Old Trafford. With the Tests at Trent Bridge and Lord's drawn, neither team had yet established an advantage, but when we got to the ground we realised this match was bound to produce a result. The pitch was very, very dry with quite a few cracks in it, even before a ball was bowled, and it was bound to get worse during the heatwave that was smothering Britain. The general feeling was that spin would be the key, and we included Albert Padmore, the off-break bowler, while England had Pat Pocock and Derek Underwood as their spinners with no one faster than the medium-pace of Mike Hendrick and Mike Selvey. As it turned out, the bowlers with genuine speed were the ones who proved the most difficult since the ball would fly once it hit a crack. So we bowled an 'Australian' length, a lot shorter than we normally would on a typically green English pitch. This prompted a lot of severely critical comment in the press about intimidatory bowling, especially late on the third day when we went after the aging England opening pair, the left-handers John Edrich, then thirty-nine, and Brian Close, forty-five. Both were hit several times about the body and the press collectively threw its hands in the air and cried 'foul'.

My argument was that if the selectors didn't feel they should be out there, they shouldn't have chosen them. But England have always been well known for depending on older players in time of need. Their hero against the Australians in the previous year was David Steele who was brought into the Test team for the first time at the age of thirty-four. Prematurely grey and wearing spectacles, he looked ten years older but he defied Lillee and Thomson and also took a century off us in the first Test. So there was no question of respecting our elders as far as Edrich and Close were concerned. More than a bad press, however, we had to acknowledge that, even though we had shaken up both batsmen, we didn't actually get either of them out that Saturday afternoon. So Clive Lloyd had a meeting with us overnight and suggested we pitch the ball up more, instructions that had an immediate effect when we resumed on the Monday as both were quickly clean bowled.

Pitches throughout that summer were drier and generally much faster than usual and clearly helped us. None was quicker than that at Abbeydale Park in Sheffield against Yorkshire when Wayne Daniel bowled like lightning, as he could when he got everything together. We had trouble ourselves against Chris Old, the Yorkshire and England pacer, who took seven for 42 as we toppled for 103 in our first innings and, in the end, the county needed to score only 110 to win. But Daniel blasted them away with six for 21. I took three for 32 in support and they could only manage a total of 90. It was the type of pitch all fast bowlers would love to take around with them in their kit bags and certainly the fastest I ever came across in England.

The victory over England went a long way towards erasing the memory of the defeat in Australia and I returned home full of enthusiasm to await the strong Pakistanis, scheduled to arrive in the Caribbean early in 1977. It was, indeed, a wonderful series between two exciting and evenly matched teams but I didn't bowl a ball in it. All I could do was follow it on the radio at home in Jamaica as my season lasted only ten overs into our first match against Barbados before I tore the rotary muscle in my right shoulder. The doctor reckoned I could have strained it with the effort in the Oval Test and I did notice some discomfort in the trials leading up to the home season. I paid little notice until it went altogether and I could hardly raise my right arm. Daniel was in the same boat, an injury also ruling him out for the season, and there was real cause for concern that our fast attack, which had done so well in England, would be badly depleted against a Pakistan team very strong in batting with players like Zaheer Abbas, Majid Khan, Asif Iqbal and the Mohammad brothers, Mushtaq and Sadiq.

As it turned out, it was a blessing in disguise. In

our absence, two big fast bowlers suddenly came on the scene to take our places, making dramatic starts to what became outstanding Test careers. Colin Croft took a record 33 wickets in the five Tests at an average of 23, including a phenomenal eight for 29 in the first innings in the second Test; and Joel Garner's return was 25 wickets at an average of 27.

By the time the series reached Jamaica, it was level 1–1 with Sabina Park hosting the decisive fifth and final Test. It was a tremendous match, the West Indies winning in the end by 140 runs. By then, however, I had more to occupy my thoughts than a match in which I wasn't playing. I had signed a contract to play cricket for an Australian by the name of Kerry Packer.

CHAPTER 6

The Packer years

The telephone call that changed my life came one March afternoon in 1977. It was Clive Lloyd on the line from Trinidad telling of plans to start what he termed 'private enterprise' cricket in Australia. It would be a series involving Australia and a World team organised, operated and financed by someone whose name didn't mean a thing to me at the time. Neither did I have a clue about why the venture was being undertaken, nor of its background.

Clive said that he, Andy Roberts and Viv Richards had been approached during the Trinidad Test against Pakistan and that he and Roberts had already signed contracts while Richards said he needed time to think about it. He did not try to influence me one way or the other but simply asked me to keep it quiet, not to mention it to anyone (although I did discuss it briefly with my parents) and to meet with two representatives of the organization who were scheduled to come to Jamaica the following week. He identified them as Tony Greig and Austin Robertson and I'm sure he detected the shock in my response to the former name. Greig, after all, had said some uncomplimentary things about us the previous summer. In any case, he was England captain and surely an establishment man. Clive's reply was, as always, level-headed. Just hear what they have to say, he suggested. That would not be necessary, I replied.

Once he and Andy were satisfied and had signed that was good enough for me. I would sign too.

When Greig and Robertson got to Jamaica, I duly met them at their hotel, the Sheraton, and they gave me chapter and verse on the scheme of Kerry Packer to launch World Series Cricket. They presented detailed figures of Packer's vast assets, explained that he owned Channel Nine, the largest television network in Australia, which would cover the matches, and said that they were recruiting the best players in the world on his behalf.

At first I only had one question. Was this for real? They assured me it was but I expressed further concern when I noticed several South Africans among the names on their list. I've always held strong views about South Africa and its apartheid policies and was conscious that the Jamaican Prime Minister of the day, Michael Manley, did so as well. I told them I could not play alongside South Africans in a World team unless, and until, they cleared it with Manley and they agreed to let me sign my contract, there and then, on that understanding. Eventually Packer did consult Manley and they reached a compromise by which only those South Africans who had played *county* cricket would be engaged. This eliminated Graeme Pollock, the great left-handed batsman who would certainly have been a draw card, and Denis Hobson, a leg-spinner whom no-one had heard much about.

I signed for three years at a fee of A$25,000 a year, which was more than four times what I had received for our tour of England the previous year. Greig and Robertson left with the promise that they would send the signing-on fee of one-third the amount to my bank account as soon as they got back to Australia. Even then, I had my doubts about it. There was no publicity in the press, no talk even among the players when they were in Jamaica for the last Test of the series. Even though Lloyd and Greig had emphasised the need for secrecy, I was sure there would be some hint of it if it was genuine. I felt it was almost impossible for something as big as this, involving so many players from so many countries, not to get to the media before long. Yet it didn't and I was only convinced it was authentic when the bank confirmed that my signing-on fee had been deposited by transfer from Australia, appreciably swelling my modest savings account.

I was completely unprepared for the explosion that was to rock the cricket world when Packer's plans did become public. I looked on it from a personal and West Indian perspective and, as far as I was aware, there was no clash between the planned Test series and Packer cricket. For others there was a conflict, and the authorities in Australia and England, especially, saw it as a direct threat. Quickly the confrontation became bitter and war broke out between the Packer group and the establishment, a war in which the West Indies Cricket Board of Control (WICBC) eventually found itself embroiled after succumbing to pressure from fellow members of the International Cricket Conference (ICC).

Packer's response to the frenzied opposition revealed a lot about the man himself and the enormous financial resources he had at his command. He simply decided to expand the operation beyond its original concept of Australia against a World team and, by the time World Series Cricket got going, in late November 1977, he had gathered more than fifty players in two Australian teams, a West Indies team and a World team, among them just about all of the cream of the crop. Almost every day, there would be news or rumours about new signings and, by the time it got going, there were sixteen West Indians, including eleven who toured England in 1976 and nine of the team that played the final Test against Pakistan in Jamaica earlier in the year. Only Alvin Kallicharran and Colin Croft were missing and Croft was to join in the second year. All the best Australians, with the exception of Jeff Thomson, were there as were some top Englishmen (Greig, Alan Knott, John Snow, Dennis Amiss, Derek Underwood, Bob Woolmer), and Pakistanis (Zaheer Abbas, Majid Khan, Asif Iqbal, Mushtaq Mohammad and Imran Khan) and the South Africans from the county circuit (Eddie Barlow, Barry Richards, Mike Procter). Only India and New Zealand were unrepresented.

Whatever the authorities and the traditionalists felt about the venture, there was no doubt about the players' attitude – and not only those contracted. Richie Benaud was very heavily involved in the operation and was one of the TV commentators. Sir Gary Sobers, Lance Gibbs and Freddie Trueman, three other former great players, also joined in various capacities. Among some of those who didn't get selected, past and present, I detected a certain amount of jealousy.

I was certainly excited by the prospect of participating in something new which promised the best cricket possible in a country I had grown so fond of on our tour in 1975–76. It also gave us, as a West Indies team, the chance to avenge ourselves and show our true worth. We had most of the players from that series but we were now older and more mature. Following our victories over India, England and Pakistan we were also more confident.

The two years of World Series Cricket proved even tougher and more innovative than I anticipated. Since the main cricket grounds were unavailable to him because of the opposition of the established State boards, Packer had go to elsewhere – to the huge VFL Park, a vast stadium located in the extreme suburbs of Melbourne, some forty-five minutes from the city centre, and the West Lakes Stadium in Adelaide, both Australian rules football facilities, and to the Exhibition Showground in Sydney and the Gloucester Park race course in Perth. As none of these had a cricket square, Packer had his own constructed in concrete trays in hothouses and then laid in the middle. He introduced cricket under lights at VFL Park, which already had them installed, using a white ball with black sightscreens. He put teams in coloured uniforms for the one-day matches that proved the popular highlight of the exercise. The Channel Nine television coverage, with nine cameras concentrated on the action, set new standards as did the cricket itself which was only to be expected with such a galaxy of stars assembled.

Still, for the first year and into the second, crowds were poor. It was an unreal feeling playing in front of a few hundred spectators at VFL Park, with its capacity of 80,000, and some of us were worried that, in spite of a lively promotional campaign, Packer was losing the propaganda war to the establishment which had the media firmly on its side.

World Series Cricket was mocked at every opportunity. Its novel publicity material, with slogans such as 'Big Boys Play at Night' and 'See the white ball fly!', was laughed at, the coloured gear referred to as pyjamas, there were veiled suggestions that the matches were fixed, and it got to a ludicrous stage where some supposedly reputable writers even claimed that the Australian Test team was stronger without its Packer men, among whom were the Chappell brothers, Dennis Lillee, Doug Walters, Rodney Marsh, Max Walker and Gary Gilmour.

At one point during the first year, an alert photographer clicked us watching the simultaneous official Test between India and Australia on the dressing-room TV set and a story appeared under the picture suggesting that Packer's West Indians preferred watching 'real' cricket! We became accustomed to all this and heeded Packer's assertion: 'It's not lack of money that will determine the future of World Series Cricket. It's the standard of play.' And Packer himself insisted on that standard.

We had heard he was a hard-nosed businessman and, having made that sort of investment, he paid close attention to it. He came to most of the matches and there was never any doubt he was in control, nor any doubt about what he demanded. After we played well below par in one of our early matches, he stormed into our dressing-room and gave us a real 'roasting'. He told us he wasn't impressed with our display and that, for the kind of money we were getting, he expected a more professional performance. We had to train harder and concentrate more. He let us know in no uncertain terms that he was going to make sure we didn't let him down. When he left the room, no-one spoke for a while. We were too stunned. Here was an Australian ticking us off because we had done badly – and against Australia at that!

Throughout, the itinerary was strenuous. In the first year, we played all over the country, not only in the big cities but in small country towns such as Rockhampton, Bendigo and Mildura. Packer wanted to propagate the gospel of his cricket and he had plenty of players at his disposal. It meant a lot of air travel and, as many of the grounds we used were a long way from city centres, long drives to and from matches as well. We alternated between 'Supertests' of four or five days and the one-day matches which formed a large part of the schedule. When we played at night, we would get back to the hotel in the early hours of the morning, dog-tired and with our metabolism completely upset by the restructuring of meal times.

In the second year, the so-called Supertests were also played under lights and comprised four days, each of seven-and-a-half hours, from two in the afternoon to ten-thirty at night. It was a gruelling exercise. What is more, there were no easy matches, such as you get on a normal tour when you play the state or county teams between Tests. You were always up against the best and, since Packer put up prize money for every match, the pressure was always on to win. Even that was denounced by the knockers who called it 'commercialism'. The players called it incentive and we finished up with an additional A$70,000 to share around after the first season.

We were not only well paid but well looked after. We stayed in top-class hotels and players were encouraged to bring their wives and families whose passages, in some cases, were paid for by the Packer organization. A VIP area was created at every ground where players' families and guests were accommodated and looked after like royalty. This treatment was previously unheard-of. In fact, the official boards had actively discouraged wives coming on tour and, certainly in the West Indies, made no provision for them at the ground. Packer knew about personnel management and was always approachable on any subject to the captain or manager. For once, the players were made to feel that they were respected for more than just their ability to make runs and take wickets and we appreciated it. It is a pity the official boards did not take heed of the example, instead of looking for ways to pull Packer down.

WSC was the making of the West Indies team of the 1980s. It toughened us up, physically as well as psychologically, and made us develop a more professional approach. Packer's early lecture left us in no doubt as to what to expect. Dr Rudi Webster was appointed our manager. A Barbadian, and a former county cricketer for Warwickshire who specialised in sports psychology, he had made quite a reputation for himself in Melbourne sporting circles in Australia. Our physiotherapist, Dennis Waight, came from the tough sport of rugby league, and significantly improved our fitness.

Dennis demanded total commitment at training sessions and never tolerated slackers. This instilled a new sense of discipline in the team, and it was the start of an important association with the tough, likeable little Aussie which has lasted ever since to the benefit of West Indies cricket. Fitness is an aspect of the game that had been given little attention until then and other countries were somewhat late in appreciating it and following our example. Now everyone places emphasis on the preparation of the players. Its effect was perhaps most noticeable in England's unexpected performance on their tour of the West Indies in 1990 following weeks of tough physical work at special pre-tour camps.

We previously did very little physical work. We just went out and played. Dennis had us on the field an hour-and-a-half before play, engaged in his special stretching and loosening up exercises. It certainly minimised the number of pulled and strained muscles and made us a lot stronger and more supple. I think, too, Dennis' strict discipline and tough regimen were psychologically good for the team as a whole, ideally complementing Clive Lloyd's approach.

There was another factor that brought all the Packer players closer together. The negative reaction of most administrators, the press and the dyed-in-the-wool traditionalists amounted to downright hostility in most cases and made us realise we were fighting for our very survival.

At first, the West Indies Board did not ban the Packer

players from Test selection, as the other countries did, so we returned from the first season of World Series Cricket to meet a badly depleted Australian team in an official Test series at home. Bobby Simpson, at the age of forty-one, had been called out of retirement to lead the Aussies in the crisis, but it was obviously a mismatch and the West Indies coasted to victory in the first two Tests in Trinidad and Barbados.

The shoulder injury that had kept me out of the Pakistan series the previous season flared up again in Australia and ruled me out of contention, but I was aware of the rumblings of discontent in the Packer players' relationships with the West Indies Board from the time we got back home. The question of our availability for a scheduled tour of India later in the year brought matters to a head. While the Packer organization was trying to arrange an accommodation that would allow the contracted players to be available, the Board kept pressuring us for a reply and set a deadline. Using that as their reason, the selectors decided to drop Deryck Murray, who was secretary of our Players' Association, and Desmond Haynes and Richard Austin, who were in their first series and had signed with WSC only a few weeks earlier. There was no question that all three deserved their places on merit and, on a matter of principle, Clive Lloyd resigned the captaincy. He was immediately followed by every Packer player who supported him to the hilt by their withdrawals.

The schism did not surprise me. Even though I was not close to the centre of the action, I had been kept constantly informed of developments by Joel Garner and could see it coming from the start. I was completely in agreement with Clive's action and, in the circumstances, would have expected nothing less from someone I respected as a man of principle.

At that stage, none of us knew whether we would

ever play Test cricket again. Personally, I wasn't convinced my Test career would last much longer anyway. In fact, had it not been for Kerry Packer, I would not have played the game for as long as I did. There was no money in it before he came along, and it offered me no great future as a career since I wasn't interested then in professional cricket in England or in becoming a full-time coach at home. I was looking in other directions to make a living and had already done a year of the computer science course at the University of the West Indies when Greig and Robertson came along with their offer of a contract. Had it not been for that, cricket would have taken a back seat in my scheme of things while I pursued another profession. And if my time in international cricket had come to an end at that point, I don't believe I would have sat around moping about it, much as I loved the game.

As it was, the second season of Packer cricket in 1978–79 proved to be such a success that it seemed to have established itself as a permanent fixture on the Australian cricket calendar. Even against the counter-attraction of a simultaneous Ashes Test series between Australia and England, crowds started to flock to the matches. Perhaps Australians were put off by the drubbing their emaciated Test team was receiving at the hands of Mike Brearley's England side but there were other reasons. Certainly one was a stepped-up promotional campaign highlighted by a lively jingle with a catch-line 'Come on, Aussie, come on' that swept the country and actually reached no. 1 on the hit-parade.

The initial adverse reaction to what many people saw as a challenge to tradition had diminished by that second year and the Test grounds in both Sydney and Brisbane became available for our use. Through Packer's backing, six gigantic light pylons were installed at the Sydney Cricket Ground (SCG) where the first night match on 28 November 1978, filled the place to overflowing. We had already played under lights but only at VFL Park. The SCG, on the other hand, was one of cricket's most famous grounds and, even though I was unable to play because of another injury that kept me out of much of that season, the thrill of that night will always remain with me. An estimated 50,000 people, caught up in the excitement, turned out and it was a truly stunning spectacle. The only thing that put us off was that we lost a low-scoring match (all out for 128 to the Australians' 129 for five) and the ghastly colour of the gear they chose for us. It was aptly described in one of the papers as 'pansy pink' and we didn't think it was such a good idea to have hefty West Indian men with macho images parading around in a distinctly unmasculine pastel shade. My injury, a snapped hamstring in the opening Supertest against the World team, kept me out for a month and when I tried to come back near the end of the season, it still wasn't healed and I had to withdraw again. At least it meant I never had to be bedecked in the pink outfit, the life of which was very brief.

That first SCG floodlit match was the night when Packer finally, and conclusively, gained the acceptance of the Australian public for which he had fought so hard. He had already won the bitter and expensive legal battle in a British High Court when Justice Slade ruled against the International Cricket Conference (ICC) decision to ban his players from their Test and domestic cricket. But I am sure Kerry Packer craved recognition for his cricket more.

He also wanted exclusive rights to televise cricket in Australia and that, as we came to understand it, was the reason for the creation of World Series Cricket, just as it was for its demise after its second season. The right to broadcast Test cricket had previously been the exclusive preserve of the government-owned Australian Broadcasting Corporation (ABC) and Packer was angry and frustrated when the Australian Board refused to give Channel Nine the rights, even though he offered to pay substantially more. The eventual accommodation involved Packer folding WSC in exchange for the TV rights, his original demand.

CHAPTER 7

World dominance

Most people in the West Indies saw Kerry Packer as a godsend for our cricketers who, they recognised, were being paid a proper wage for the first time. They could not understand what was the difference between us signing up for WSC and signing up for an Australian state or an English county. We were pursuing our profession and the majority saw the ICC's ruling just as Justice Slade had done, as a restraint of trade.

Since the organisers made sure televised highlights of the matches went back to the West Indies, there was tremendous interest, and the natural follow-up was a series in the Caribbean between WSC Australia and WSC West Indies in 1979. West Indians had been denied the chance of seeing the strongest Australian team the year before and they looked forward to this series with keen anticipation. They had not forgotten our 5–1 loss to much the same team in Australia in 1975–76 and wanted us to set the balance right. The Chappell brothers, Rodney Marsh and the four fast bowlers of that series, headed by Lillee and Thomson, were in Packer's team. But we were now stronger and had proved ourselves time and again since the 1975–76 debâcle. In the Supertests in Australia, honours were even. We had a 2–1 edge in the first year but had been soundly beaten by ten wickets at the SCG the following season after drawing the first match at VFL Park. We arrived back in the West Indies with everything to play for.

The official West Indies team, captained by Alvin Kallicharran, was just ending a Test series in India where, not surprisingly, they had struggled. Back home, there was still animosity in official quarters to Packer but we got sponsorship from Neal and Massey, one of the Caribbean's largest companies, and secured the Test grounds of Sabina Park in Jamaica, Kensington Oval in Barbados, the Queen's Park Oval in Trinidad, Bourda in Guyana and the Recreation Ground in Antigua for the five Supertests. Throughout, we attracted good crowds and also visited several of the Windward and Leeward Islands for one-day matches which made the schedule every bit as hectic and demanding as in Australia.

The contest was keenly and evenly fought. The only two outright results were at Sabina Park in the first Supertest and at the Queen's Park Oval in the third. We won in Jamaica by 369 runs when Lloyd hit a magnificent 197. The Australians won by 24 runs in a cliff-hanger on a typically difficult pitch in Trinidad in which Bruce Laird, the dogged little opener, made 122 and Greg Chappell scored 150 in a match in which the highest total was 282. There was a lot of good cricket throughout and I had the chance to make up for missing a lot of both seasons in Australia through injury. However, by the time the Caribbean series started I was fully recovered and was pleased with my performance, taking 24 wickets in the five matches at an average of 20.79. All sportsmen fear injury more than failure but I tried to be philosophical about mine. Perhaps it was because I had to deal with so many that I adopted the attitude of what will be, will be. My concern was always more for the effect my absence would have on the team than for myself personally since I knew I would be able to find a job back in Jamaica fairly readily if it ever came to that. I was lucky that we always had such great fast bowling reserves to fill the gap and that Clive Lloyd and my teammates were supportive and understanding whenever I broke down. All the same, it was very depressing just watching from the pavilion, and it was a relief to be able to run up and bowl throughout the WSC tour of the West Indies without any physical restriction.

Unfortunately the series was spoiled by the rain that kept following us everywhere and by the crowd trouble that erupted in Barbados and Guyana. Neither were new to West Indies cricket but we certainly got more of both than we would have liked. And they were not unrelated.

When play was delayed because of wet outfields in both matches, spectators were kept waiting with no word from officials on the public address system as to why they were seeing no cricket or when they could expect some. There seemed no official direction and when the crowd's patience snapped, violence broke out. In Barbados, we got playing after the first disturbance only for the match to be finally halted when Roy Fredericks was given out lbw, a decision the fans didn't like and which brought another rain of bottles on to the ground. In Guyana, the situation was even worse. The people pushed over fences and streamed across the ground to storm the old wooden Georgetown Cricket Club pavilion where both teams, trapped in the insecure dressing-rooms, took shelter how we could. Several picked up their bats to use as defensive weapons in case of invasion and donned helmets as protection. I just sat on a bench and hoped for the best. But I won't pretend it wasn't a frightening experience, cooped up in such a small area, not knowing just where the crowd's anger would carry it. Luckily, apart from Collis King, who was slightly cut by flying glass, no-one was hurt before the furore subsided.

Of course WSC's detractors had a field day. They claimed it all demonstrated the people's subconscious opposition to the series even though such claims were refuted by the size of the attendances everywhere. But it was true that the organization, often in the hands of people lacking experience in administration, left a lot to be desired.

There was repeated speculation throughout the tour that the Australian Board and Packer had reached some agreement that would mean the end of WSC. We knew they had been talking but rumour had become so much part of the whole business that I preferred to wait for official confirmation. What I did know was that things were going so well for WSC now that whatever agreement was reached would have to be on Packer's terms.

About a month after the series in the Caribbean ended, the news came that a truce had been signed by which Packer would wind up his cricket in exchange for the exclusive television coverage of Test cricket in Australia. If he had been granted it in the first place, he would not have needed to set up his own circuit, the revolution that turned the game on its head would never have taken place, and I might well have become a very diligent computer programmer with the Jamaica Government.

While Packer's operation was over, the wounds it opened were deep and raw and the scars would remain for some time. There had been division not just between WSC and the established boards but even between the non-Packer and Packer players. The England team in Pakistan declared it would not play against WSC contractees if they were chosen when they went back home for the series in 1977–78, and their Cricketers' Association passed motions to keep them out of county cricket. In Australia, they were even debarred from club cricket.

Even though the stand-off was officially over by the time the second World Cup came around in England in June 1979, Australia and England refused to pick any of their Packer men. We never encountered such opposition in the West Indies and, while the rift did develop between the players and the Board over the question of selection during the Australian series of 1978, the Board was constantly under pressure from the public and never seemed comfortable with the situation. With matters resolved in Australia, our selectors were quick to choose the best team to defend the World Cup in England in 1979.

We were very much as we were. Clive Lloyd was reinstated as captain, and Deryck Murray as vice-captain, and only four of the squad of fifteen came from the West Indies team that toured India and Sri Lanka for the official Test series in 1978–79. Among them was Alvin Kallicharran who had taken over as captain when Clive resigned. It was obvious that 'Kalli' felt he had been hard done by as he was relegated to the ranks again and, even though it was a naive and unrealistic attitude, it was one he never overcame. He was the only one of the non-Packer players to make the final eleven in the World Cup which remained the same right through. The other three non-Packer players, Larry Gomes, Faoud Bacchus and Malcolm Marshall, remained in the reserves.

The team was now maturing together. Most of us had gone into WSC with only a few years of international cricket and two or three tours behind us and, since Roy Fredericks retired after the second season to go into politics in Guyana, the only remaining over-30s were the captain and vice-captain. They were two knowledgeable and respected cricketers in the leadership positions.

The quality and quantity of the cricket we played in Australia gave us a sharp edge and we were a closely knit unit under Lloyd. We were certain of ourselves, were fit, strong in every department and played for each other. For the next four or five years, we were to enjoy the most successful period of any West Indies team in history.

There were other reasons for our dominance. We had such a settled side that we went through series after series having to call on no more than twelve or thirteen players. Our 1979 World Cup squad was Lloyd, Deryck Murray, Gordon Greenidge, Desmond Haynes, Viv Richards, Alvin Kallicharran, Collis King, Andy Roberts, Joel Garner, Colin Croft, Larry Gomes, Faoud Bacchus, Malcolm Marshall and myself, and these remained the nucleus of the team for much of the next decade.

This provided a consistency of selection that is so vital in any team sport. Additionally, England and Australia became like second homes to our players. The majority had played county or league cricket in England for some time and Greenidge had not only been raised there but came into the first-class game with Hampshire. Until I finally took the plunge and committed myself to full-time professional cricket in 1981, I was the odd man out, the only regular member of the Test team not contracted to an English club.

The two successive seasons with WSC familiarised us with Australia. If you don't have your head screwed on the first time you go there, you can get carried away with the extra-curricular diversions. I saw that happen in 1975–76 and I've heard enough stories to know that it had upset earlier touring teams as well. So we came to know those countries where we would play most often and with whom we had the closest rivalry almost as well as we knew the Caribbean – their grounds, their conditions, their opponents, their umpires, their crowds and their lifestyles. It is a big advantage to any touring team.

In the circumstances, it was hardly surprising that we easily retained the World Cup. Both England and Australia chose not to pick their Packer men and it is pertinent that our toughest match was the semi-final against Pakistan who did include theirs. We advanced by beating India and New Zealand in the first round but, even though we were well placed with a total of 293 for six off our 60 overs in the semi-final at The Oval, Pakistan were threatening when Majid Khan and Zaheer Abbas, two of their Packer players, added 166 for the second wicket on an Oval pitch which hadn't changed its character all that much since 1976. It was a lovely, sunny summer's day and runs were flowing far too easily for our liking when Lloyd brought back Croft. He instructed him to bowl a leg-stump line, with his in-slanting angle of delivery, since both Majid and Zaheer were very strong off-side batsmen. It was a clever piece of captaincy and Croft quickly had Zaheer caught by Murray down the leg-side and also dismissed Majid and Javed Miandad to ease our worries.

Our opponents in the final were England, a team always to be respected in one-day cricket of which they get so much experience. With the benefit of bowling first on an overcast morning, they took the early honours and, when Chris Old held a good return catch to dismiss Lloyd, we were struggling at 99 for four. Whenever we're in trouble, I tend not to watch and this habit caused me to miss what everyone reported later was some of the most daring strokeplay I could have hoped to see. If I and others were worried, Viv Richards and Collis King obviously were not. They took over Lord's with a partnership that added 139 in an hour-and-a-quarter and England's usually unflustered captain, Mike Brearley, admitted afterwards he 'felt powerless' to do anything about it.

By now, Viv had no peer among the game's batsmen. Quite apart from his natural ability, he exuded a sense of superiority which allowed him to impose himself on bowlers as soon as he walked to the wicket and, like all great batsmen, he had the habit of producing runs when they mattered most and frequently on the big occasion. This was an unusual innings in that he subjected himself to playing second fiddle to King. Collis was a very strong man with powerful arms and shoulders and keen eyesight. If his technique was unorthodox and somewhat loose, he could 'murder' bowling on a flat pitch such as Lord's was that day. He could also bowl a bit at medium pace and was a dynamic fielder but, as a carefree individual with a love of the good things of life, he lacked the self-discipline required at the highest level. He could not hold down a permanent place in the Test side before going off to South Africa in 1983 but, on that June day, Lord's was his as he hit 86 off 67 balls with three big sixes and ten fours.

England were shell-shocked by the time they got him out and Viv took over to finish with 138 not out, flicking Mike Hendrick's last ball off his toes over square-leg for six, one of the few shots of his I did see. We knew 286 for nine would take a lot of getting and when Brearley and Geoff Boycott overdid their job of laying a solid base to England's reply, the Cup was all but ours again. Boycott took something like seventeen overs to get into double-figures and some of my West Indian friends swore to me afterwards that Clive Lloyd deliberately dropped a dolly at mid-off just to keep him in. A good start is important in one-day cricket, especially when the overs are as many as sixty as they were in that World Cup. But the batsmen have got to know when, and how, to change gear as Viv did so expertly early in the day. By the time I came back for my second spell, the pressure was on England and, after I dismissed both Brearley and Boycott, Garner demolished the rest of the innings with his speciality, the yorker, bowling four of his five victims.

It was a thrill to retain the official world championship at a packed Lord's. The ground still retains that aura as the mecca of cricket and it seemed, that day, that all the unpleasantness surrounding Packer cricket had never occurred. It was a thrill, as well, to learn that the Australian Board had altered its programme and that we would be returning there for the 1979–80 season, along with England, for three Tests and a one-day series. It was all part of the deal the Australians had worked out with Packer and, as it challenged the traditional format, it came in for a lot of criticism. As far as I was concerned, it was a chance to get back to Australia while the team was at its peak with both the Australians and ourselves able to call on all our players in an officially recognised series. As we were sharing the season with England we had only three Tests each, but we were anxious to put 1975–76 behind us and this tour would allow us to prove a point.

CHAPTER 8

Together again

The new structure of Australian cricket was established in the first season after the disbandment of Packer cricket. There would be two Test series of three matches each, against England and the West Indies, with a three-way series of one-day internationals for the Benson & Hedges World Series Cup contested in between. There would be prize money, Man of the Match and Man of the Series awards, night cricket, white balls, the lot.

It was all too much for the Englishmen to take and they baulked at almost all the innovations, with the exception of the prize money. They never advanced any convincing arguments against, say, coloured stripes on their white shirts and trousers or the introduction of the field-restricting area to eliminate ultra-defensive tactics, but they weren't about to let the Aussies usurp any of their power.

For us it was an enjoyable and triumphant season – and profitable as well since we finished up with just over A$100,000 in prize money in the kitty to add to our fee. Yet it didn't start all that well. We lost our first two one-day internationals, the first to Australia and the second to England, both under lights at the SCG which over the next few years developed into our bogey ground. At least the loss to England had one beneficial side-effect. On England's insistence, there was no limitation on field placing, so their captain, Mike Brearley, was free to place everyone on the boundary to prevent Colin Croft, our no. 11, hitting the boundary off the last ball from Ian Botham we needed to win the match. That was bad enough, but Brearley carried it to the extreme by instructing David Bairstow, the bemused wicketkeeper, to drop back to the fence as well. The SCG spectators let the 'Poms' know exactly how they felt about this abomination. Even most of the England boys were embarrassed by it. The press also had a go and the field-restricting area, ensuring that there are at least four fielders within the 30-metres zone at all times, has been part of the one-day rules ever since.

Immediately after that second defeat, we learned that Clive Lloyd would be unavailable for the first Test at Brisbane which followed in a few days. He had complained of pain in his knees for some time and had already had a cartilage operation on his left one. Now the right knee needed attention. Although he assured us that, with modern surgical techniques, he would be back playing within a week or so, this was hard to believe. His absence, and rumours circulating that his tour, and even his career, might have been over sent us into that Test a little bit down although I wouldn't give that as the reason we failed to convert a strong first-innings position into victory. The pitch became easier and easier and Greg Chappell and Kim Hughes got second-innings centuries, Greg 124, Kim 134 not out, and Bruce Laird, the plucky little opener from Perth who had shown his courage over and over in WSC, did so again with two long knocks of 92 and 75. Yet it is impossible to overestimate the esteem in which Clive was held by the team, and an operation such as he was to undergo was bound to be cause for concern.

As it was, the surgery did the magic Clive promised it would and, amazingly, he was back at the helm within a fortnight, well in time to lead us to successive victories in the last two Tests at Melbourne and Adelaide and in the one-day competition as well. It was the first time the West Indies had ever won a Test series in Australia, or even won more than a single Test, and there could be no disputing the quality of our performance.

We came within 22 runs of winning by an innings in Melbourne, taking it by ten wickets in four days, and the margin in Adelaide was even greater, by 408 runs, one of the biggest in Test history. The fact that Australia completed a clean sweep over England by easily winning all three Tests of their series underlined just how strong we were and how well we played.

It was good to be back in traditional cricket, representing the united West Indies again and showing our true worth. Packer cricket was a tremendous experience that served us well. We made a lot of money, won a lot of matches and became very popular with Australian crowds. But, strong and competitive as it was, it was one half of a divided cricket world. Now the game was united again and everyone back to full strength.

We used only twelve players in the three Tests and would have kept an unchanged team but for Clive's enforced absence from the first Test. The Australians, on the other hand, called on eighteen players. Our fast attack was settled and well established, with Andy Roberts and myself sharing the new ball and Joel Garner and Colin Croft first and second change. I was happy with the way I was bowling and more so with my fitness. I was no longer bothered by the injuries that had affected me so frequently before Dennis Waight arrived and put us through his running and stretching exercises and weight training routine.

Dickie Bird, the umpire, described my run-up as 'Whispering Death'. I never carried much weight, was light on my feet, and I didn't pound the turf on the way in. (*Patrick Eagar*)

'Mikey' at six months (*above, left*); and managing a few unsteady early steps at the family home on Dunrobin Avenue, Kingston; (*below*) My first cricket tour – with the Melbourne Club to the Cayman Islands. I am standing fifth from right. My father, Ralph, is ninth from right. Flanking me are two of my early coaches, Bruce Wellington and Teddy Griffith (third and sixth from right respectively).

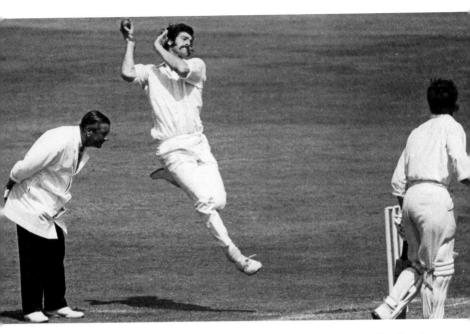

Dennis Lillee (*above*) has been an inspiration to a whole generation of fast bowlers. See his perfect poise as he moves into the delivery stride in the 1972 Lord's Test. (*Below, left*) Ian Chappell, a batsman who was always a challenge. (*Below, right*) I have not seen anyone make batting look simpler than Lawrence Rowe, on his way here to a century against Australia at Brisbane, 1975–76. (*Patrick Eagar*)

(*Above*) Andy Roberts and I warm up on a Brighton beach early in the 1976 tour of England in which each of us took 28 wickets in the series. (*Daily Mirror*); (*below*) Ken Kelly's photograph shows Andy, a truly great fast bowler, in the delivery stride, while Patrick Eagar's study of my action was made at The Oval where I took 14 wickets.

(*Above*) The most satisfying of those 14 wickets – Tony Greig bowled leg stump for 1 in the second innings at The Oval. (*Patrick Eagar*)
(*Below*) One of the Kerry Packer innovations: cricket under lights at VFL Park, Melbourne, in the first year of World Series Cricket. (*PBL Marketing*)

(*Above*) World Cup Champions, 1979. Seated, Holding, Kallicharran, Deryck Murray, Lloyd (captain), Walcott (manager), Richards, Roberts, Greenidge. Standing: Bacchus, Gomes, Marshall, Garner, Croft, King, Haynes. (*Ken Kelly*)
(*Below*) The pace quartet: Garner, Croft, Roberts and Holding at Adelaide, third Test, 1980. (*Patrick Eagar*)

(*Above*) Boycott, b Holding, 0. Third Test, West Indies v. England, Bridgetown, 1981. (*Below*) No pain, no gain. Here am I at Lord's, stretched out with Colin Croft (*centre*) and Andy Roberts at the start of the 1981 tour of England. (*Patrick Eagar*)

The splendour of Sabina Park. The view is from the George Headley stand towards

The star of the season was, again and unquestionably, Viv Richards. He had long since proven himself the best batsman in the world as well as the most exciting and commanding. Now he outdid himself. He started with a century in the first Test, 140 at Brisbane, and followed with 96 at Melbourne and 76 and 74 at Adelaide. Throughout the one-day matches, he batted consistently and brilliantly.

Everyone marvelled at his unbeaten century in the World Cup final at Lord's the previous summer but even that couldn't compare for sheer majesty and power with his unbeaten 153 in a one-day international at the Melbourne Cricket Ground against an Australian attack including Lillee, Thomson and their new fast bowling find, Rodney Hogg. He faced only 131 balls and lashed a six and 16 fours. Yet he was in such discomfort from a back injury that dogged him all season that he had to have pain-killing injections before going out and limped for most of the time.

Viv always had this phenomenal belief in his ability and, at that stage of his career, no bowler could hold him in check. An incident in the Melbourne Test typified his personality perfectly. We had bowled Australia out for 156 on the first day and he came in with less than an hour left in our first innings after Greenidge was out. While most batsmen would have sought to play out time, Viv attacked from the start before he was interrupted by a blow to the head when he missed a hook off Hogg. Throughout his career, he never wore a helmet and he was so shaken that Dennis Waight had to rush onto the field to administer some quick attention. When he recovered his composure and took strike again, Hogg hammered in another bouncer first ball and Viv despatched it over the long-leg boundary with a disdainful hook for six.

In my book Viv Richards truly qualifies for the

accolade of 'great' because he proved himself over an extended period everywhere, against every type of bowling, in all conditions and frequently when the team was in trouble. He was so certain of himself, he never gave failure a thought. It is a hallmark of his greatness that he would play shots that defied the textbook and yet he was just as capable of flawless orthodoxy and tight defence.

With his belief in his own ability, Viv would strut around, giving the impression of arrogance. But he didn't have to brag about how good he was. For him, actions spoke louder than words.

Playing together with him for the West Indies, I thankfully didn't have to bowl at him much. When I did, I knew I couldn't devise any specific plan to get him out as I would with most other batsmen. I would just try to bowl as tight as possible and hope for him to make a mistake. He was a genius, capable of hitting the same ball three different ways to the boundary. With such a batsman, you just try not to let him embarrass you.

Richards used his body language as part of his method of psychologically dominating the bowler. After hammering a boundary, he would saunter down the pitch and just tap it with his bat while giving the bowler an annoying smirk or fixing him with a stern glare. Whenever I bowled against him, I would either ignore him completely, not even looking at him, or else go the other route and applaud any good shots. But he upset a lot of bowlers who got uptight at his antics, none more so than Lennie Pascoe who came into the Australian team during the Packer years. Lennie had hot Czech blood pumping through his veins and it seldom took very long for him to lose his cool and start bouncing – and it wasn't very long before fine leg would be retrieving balls hit by Richards from over the fence.

In his later years, Viv had problems with his health and was not as consistent as he was in his heyday which I would put as the years between 1976 and 1981. He still tried to play the impossible shots that used to come so easily but his eyesight and reflexes were just not the same and his big scores became fewer and fewer. However, at his peak, as he was on this tour, he was incomparable.

Yet I do not regard him as the best batsman I ever saw, the emphasis being on the verb 'saw'. That accolade I still reserve for Lawrence Rowe.

Rowe was in his prime when I first came into Jamaican cricket at youth level in the early 1970s and I could not imagine anyone ever batting better or being able to. He made big scores consistently, double-centuries for Jamaica, a record of double and single centuries on his Test debut in 1972 against New Zealand in Jamaica, 302 against England in Barbados in 1974. Like all Jamaicans, I was spellbound and, in that period, what struck me most was that he never, but never, played at a ball and missed. Everything hit the middle of the bat and whatever stroke he chose to play (and he had them all) would have the desired result. His technique was superb, his eyesight like a cat's and he had all the time in the world to play with captivating ease and elegance. I have not seen such perfection since.

Whatever he did looked as if it came easily, but I know Lawrence Rowe worked very hard at his game, practising frequently and getting himself physically fit. At the age of thirty-one, this tour of Australia was his last for the West Indies, although he later led a rebel team to South Africa. The difference between himself and Viv Richards was that between a player who earned the title 'great' and one who didn't.

Rowe had a very presentable Test average in the

end, 43.55, but if he had had the strength of character and will-power of a Richards nobody could have
surpassed what he would have achieved. Instead, he
lacked the ingredients so essential for those at the
top, self-confidence and determination. When things
started to go against him, he would blame his failures
on everything but himself. It reached the stage where
he became so paranoid over the high expectations of
a public that was accustomed to his effortless high-
scoring that he was reluctant to go out to bat for fear
of failure.

At what we call in Jamaica a 'curry goat' social
match at Content Gardens in the countryside one
weekend, a large crowd turned out specially to see
Rowe. I was there along with several other island
players but it was Rowe who was the centre of
attention. His popularity was then at its zenith and he
disappointed everybody by refusing to bat. There had
been rain, the pitch was damp and he protested that,
in the conditions, he could not be the Lawrence Rowe
the people were expecting. It revealed a lot about his
personality. He was never sure of himself in spite of
his outstanding record and it inevitably affected his
cricket. But, for a few years in the early 1970s, I have
never seen anyone making batting look simpler.

Unlike Rowe, Richards and Clive Lloyd thrived when
things got rough, as Clive showed in that 1979–80 series.
He overcame his operation and a bad patch of form
to finish with a tremendous century, 121, at Adelaide
that set up the victory and erased a little self-doubt that
seemed to be surfacing about his future.

He was then thirty-six and hadn't been doing very
much with the bat when a journalist asked him at
practice prior to the Adelaide Test how much longer
he had in Test cricket. 'Maybe five days,' Clive replied.
Five days later, as we celebrated with several bottles

of the finest Australian champagne, such doubt had been firmly dispelled. We were floating on a high and the world was a wonderful place. Little did we suspect what lay waiting for us across the Tasman Sea in New Zealand.

CHAPTER 9

Trouble across the Tasman

We left for New Zealand the day after the final Test against Australia at Adelaide on 31 January 1980 and things went badly wrong from the moment we arrived at Auckland airport to the day we flew out five weeks later.

As we cleared customs, we were instructed to unpack our gear so that our boots could be inspected for any soil. When that was over, we had to lug our bags to the bus ourselves. The cramped, motel-type accommodation contrasted sharply with the five-star luxury we had come to take for granted in Australia. The food at the grounds, usually sausage and beans, was neither appetising nor filling. The weather was mostly cold and damp. It was a complete comedown after Australia, as if we had been moved from the penthouse into the basement overnight.

As I came to appreciate on later visits, it wasn't a question of being hassled as we were sure we were. *Every* team that goes to New Zealand has to have its boots inspected for soil to prevent certain agricultural diseases entering, and the country is smaller and less sophisticated than Australia. It is a long-standing Australian joke that airline captains advise their passengers to turn their watches back fifty years on the flight from Sydney to Auckland. But none of us had been there before and we were on such a high that we weren't prepared for such a change.

One thing led to another but the last and heaviest straw was the standard of the umpiring which was, without doubt or qualification, the worst I have ever seen at Test match level. It even exceeded what had taken place in Australia during the 1975–76 tour. In the three Tests, Deryck Murray estimated that two dozen clear decisions went against us, mostly for catches to him behind the wicket. I had long since stopped counting – or even appealing. The excuse was put forward that the umpires had never witnessed bowling as fast as ours and couldn't detect the edges. Such laughable talk only made things worse.

New Zealand had long been the Cinderella of world cricket and tours there were almost inevitably tacked on at the tail end of those to Australia, as this one was. They were desperate for recognition and were then building up a team that could hold its own. Their eventual victory by virtue of a one-wicket win in the first Test over opponents who were regarded as world champions was a tremendous boost to their cricket but they were only deluding themselves by achieving it this way. While they had a fair team, they were not nearly as strong as Australia. As it was, we were totally frustrated, and were never at our best, especially since Viv Richards had returned home from Australia to rest his back injury.

In such an atmosphere, the several incidents that attended the series were probably inevitable if, on reflection, regrettable. The team manager, Willie Rodriguez, told the press afterwards that we were like 'sixteen big fish in a deep, big ocean with nobody to turn to' and that we could take so much and no more. Not everyone agreed and there were serious repercussions to what surely ranks as one of the most controversial tours in cricket history. For me, it was certainly the most disagreeable.

By the time the first Test came around, the spirit we had brought from Australia had disappeared. We had been beaten by one wicket with two balls to go in a one-day international and struggled to keep in contention on the first four days of the Test. It was so cold in the South Island city of Dunedin that we spent most of the match huddled around the heater in the dressing-room. On the field, we were bowled out for 140 on the first day and finished 109 behind on first innings. Had it not been for Desmond Haynes' careful second innings of 105 we would have been nowhere. As it was, we only managed to give them 104 to win.

The tension of the match, and the prospects of victory, seemed to grip all New Zealand. Prior to the last day, the newspapers and radio stations were filled with cricket hype with one radio DJ calling us 'a bunch of whingers' and boasting that the Kiwis would make sure we got our just desserts. We were overrated, said one writer. There was no doubt we were in trouble but all the braggadocio fired us up and made us determined to go out and stuff their words back down their throats by bowling them out for under 100.

I can't remember wanting to win quite so desperately as I did that day and, when I dismissed the left-handed openers, John Wright and Bruce Edgar, cheaply I knew it was a decisive breakthrough. New Zealand depended very heavily on the top four in their order of whom Wright, captain Geoff Howarth and John Parker were all playing county cricket. After that came a long tail and when I had Parker caught behind off his glove before he had scored, we were on course for the victory we craved so much. We didn't feel they had a chance after that – and certainly no-one felt the umpire could possibly give not out. It was so clear the ball had deflected from Parker's glove to Murray that I didn't even think of looking back for a decision. I kept on running down the pitch to celebrate the wicket with Murray and the slips but when I got alongside Parker, I noticed that, even though he had his bat under his arm, was taking off his gloves and looking towards the pavilion, he wasn't moving. So I looked behind me to see what the umpire was doing. His hands were still down and, when I appealed, all I got was a sheepish smile and a shake of his head.

At that moment, I lost all control, spun around and kicked the nearest thing to me, which happened to be the off-stump at the batsman's end. The incriminating photograph has since appeared far too frequently for my liking. It shows two stumps out of the ground, the bails flying, my right foot head-high on the follow-through.

I'd been through this whole business before when umpire Ledwidge gave Ian Chappell not out at Sydney four years earlier and my immediate reaction now was the same. This was not cricket and I didn't have to be part of it. I was on my way to the pavilion, quite prepared not to bowl again, when Lloyd and Murray came across and persuaded me back. So I kept on trying and I will always consider we won that Test, whatever else *Wisden* may say. As the New Zealanders inched their way towards their target, we had a few more clear decisions given not out, right down to the last ball when an lbw shout from Garner was given as the winning leg-bye.

For me, my tour was as good as over. At the team meeting after the match, I told the others they were at liberty to do what they wanted but I had no intention of even appealing for the remainder of the series. Garner, Croft and a few of the others contended that we had to go on trying, no matter what, because we just couldn't let New Zealand beat us. It wasn't that I wasn't going to try. I simply wouldn't appeal because it was obviously going to be a waste of breath. I know they couldn't understand my attitude and probably it was extreme. But I could never put up with the sort of obvious incompetence, and injustice, that was taking place.

I was amused, therefore, when Garner very nearly stopped bowling in the next match against Wellington when he had a clear caught behind appeal turned down. In the next Test at Lancaster Park in Christchurch, he turned to me after yet another wicket had been refused and said, apologetically: 'You know, I think you're right. We're just wasting our breath.'

By then, we were going through the motions, trying not to let it get too much on top of us. But no matter how much you tell yourself not to react, no matter how you try to condition yourself that the end of the tour must come, your fuse sparks when you're in the heat of battle and bowling fast.

The pressure was building and the volcano finally erupted during the second Test at Christchurch. We lost the toss, were sent in and were three down for 28 on a green pitch before Greenidge and Kallicharran pulled us round by adding 162. After that, we collapsed to 228 all out, a score that put pressure on the bowlers again. Still, we got their first three wickets for 53 only to find our path again blocked by the umpires. Several clear-cut appeals against captain Geoff Howarth were turned down although, I might add, there was no appealing from me.

When we came off the field at tea on the third day, we were fuming. Howarth was 99 and the match had slipped from our grasp through no fault of our own. Even Clive Lloyd, who had a reputation everywhere for his calm, sensible approach to things, could not contain himself. 'Gentlemen,' he said, 'this is rubbish. We can't play cricket like this.' There and then we decided that whatever the consensus of the team it would be carried. It was no surprise when we unanimously decided not to go back on to the field again. It was an extreme and unprecedented position but we felt it had to be taken.

So we sat in the dressing-room while the umpires went back out and waited for us to follow. In a while, an official of the New Zealand Board arrived, in something of a panic, to tell us that the umpires were waiting. 'Well, they can wait but we won't be joining them,' Clive advised him. It was at that point that the message got through. In no time, Howarth appeared and, after he and Clive had gone off to another room to discuss the matter, Clive returned to tell us he had got Howarth's assurance that his players would walk without waiting for a decision once they knew they had hit the ball. That, we felt, should surely help clear things up.

So we eventually went back out, more than ten minutes late, only for Howarth, in the very first over, to stand his ground for yet another clear catch by Murray behind the wicket. After play that evening, most of us were still in favour of abandoning the match and the tour. We packed our bags and vacated the dressing-room in anticipation of an early flight out.

Back at the hotel on the rest day, the arguments raged as to whether we should continue playing or not. We told the captain we would abide by whatever he decided. Clive replied that he would rather not have to determine such an important issue by himself. He had been in the game for a long time and was nearing the end but there were younger men with plenty still ahead of them involved as well. So it went to the vote and the majority again said no more play, a decision even supported by the manager, Willie Rodriguez. However, we still had to get in touch with the West Indies Board and, after several telephone calls between Rodriguez and Board executives back home, it became clear we would have to soldier on. In hindsight, it was the sensible decision.

Not that anything improved. The very next day, there was more controversy when Croft bounced umpire Fred Goddall on his run-up after yet another astonishing decision, another not out given for a high catch to Murray as Richard Hadlee wafted at a bouncer over his head. There were howls of anguish from all over the world at what was going on. Those who were thousands of miles away, and could not possibly know what was happening, showed no sympathy for our predicament. Had we abandoned the tour, we would have been pilloried but, by being persuaded to stay, we subjected ourselves to more indignities.

On our return home, the West Indies Board, as it probably felt it had to do, issued a strong statement condemning our protests and our 'bad sportsmanship' on the tour. It demanded, and got, apologies from myself and Croft for our incidents and Clive wrote an apology on behalf of himself and the team to both the West Indies and New Zealand Boards, although he did not fail to mention that we encountered 'some very incompetent umpiring'.

'Very incompetent umpiring' has caused problems in international cricket from time immemorial and I was amused a few years later to read that the New Zealand team walked off the field in a Test match in Pakistan in 1984–85 in protest against a decision by umpire Shakoor Rana and that the manager and the captain, then Jeremy Coney, had issued an official statement sharply critical of the umpiring. It seemed poetic justice. The same Shakoor Rana was to be involved in a more highly publicised flare-up with the England captain, Mike Gatting, in a Test in Pakistan in 1988 that caused an international diplomatic incident.

Yet the authorities have sat back and done nothing about it. All other international team sports are now carried by officials from neutral countries. While the ICC has talked about setting up an international panel, and has agreed in principle to the idea, it has kept finding reasons when it would not be feasible. I believe, and almost all the modern players I have spoken to on the subject are agreed, that such a panel would go a long way to eliminating the feeling of so many visiting teams that they are being cheated. That is the crux of the matter.

The ICC's decision to appoint an independent match referee to oversee Test matches at least goes part of the way to solving the problem. But it is still not the same as having two umpires who are not only unbiased but also seen to be unbiased. The Pakistanis have twice grasped the nettle and employed English umpires, John Hampshire and John Holder, for potentially volatile home series against India, and the last two World Cups have very successfully employed the system of neutral umpires. Still the ICC continues to drag its feet.

In New Zealand, in 1980, it might not have been anything more than utter incompetence. But we felt we were being robbed left, right and centre and could do absolutely nothing about it.

CHAPTER 10

Full-time cricketer

One of the several repercussions of Kerry Packer's World Series Cricket was a sharp increase in the number of international tours and the accompanying proliferation of one-day matches, especially in Australia where the lights and the television coverage helped make them so popular.

For the West Indies, it was a matter of dollars and cents. Packer raised the pay of the players to realistic new standards and the Board had to meet a sharp increase in its expenses. Since it makes nothing from either international or domestic cricket at home and its balance sheet regularly shows a heavy loss, it has to depend on revenue from its overseas tours where crowds are bigger and rights for television high.

After WSC was dissolved following the tour of the Caribbean in April 1979, the West Indies returned to the unified fold to play virtually non-stop for the next two years. We started with the World Cup in England which was followed by the tours of Australia and New Zealand, a full tour of England in 1980, a series in Pakistan late in 1980 and England's visit to the Caribbean in February–April 1981. That made a total of nineteen Tests and heaven knows how many one-day internationals in five different countries in less than two years.

It was a schedule that wouldn't slacken and I realised that I would finally have to take the plunge and become a full-time professional cricketer. It had been dawning for some time that I couldn't, in all conscience, retain my post with the government computer department while taking as much time as I was for Jamaica and West Indies cricket. Even when I went back into the job during the brief period between tours, I found it was untenable. It requires three or four months to write a complex computer programme and I could never find that kind of time in between my cricket. It meant all I could do was update other people's material, not a particularly satisfying chore. So when I was approached in England in 1980 to join a club in the Lancashire League the following season, I didn't need much prompting.

Wilf Woodhouse, the chairman of Rishton club, must have heard of my reluctance to get into full-time pro cricket for he was a little diffident when he put forward his offer during the Old Trafford Test. 'This is only weekend league cricket,' he explained, 'nothing strenuous, so give it a thought and let me know.' I let him know the next morning and that is how I joined the ranks of full-time professional cricketers. Over the next few years, I would play for more teams in more countries than most others.

My two previous visits, in the scorching hot summer of 1976 and for the 1979 World Cup, left me wondering whether my leg had been pulled with all the stories I had heard over the years about the British weather. The 1980 season put that right. The rain dripped from cool, grey skies almost daily and the series never got going properly. It was decided in our favour by the only outright result, a hard-fought victory by two wickets at Trent Bridge, although we were never under pressure in the remaining four Tests in which we did not once bat in our second innings.

Cricket is almost pointless in such conditions. Yet the series was far from wasted from our point of view since it saw the continuing maturing of Desmond Haynes as an opening batsman, and gave Malcolm Marshall his first chance to prove himself.

Haynes first made his name with a brilliant century for the West Indies in a one-day international against Bobby Simpson's Australians in 1978. We were then shopping around for an opener to take Fredericks' place and that innings gained him the spot as Greenidge's partner that he never gave up. He had an early reputation as a flashy stroke-maker, so much so that they gave him the nickname 'Hammer Haynes' when he first went to Australia with WSC, and he developed the habit of getting out in the 30s and 40s when well set. It is a problem that faces many young batsmen.

My impression was that he had no real pressure to produce big innings since we were winning so easily. It took the difficulties of New Zealand, when our batting did struggle, for him to realise how important he could be to the team. He relished the challenge of holding the innings together against Richard Hadlee on the green top pitches and scored centuries at Dunedin and Christchurch which transformed him into a responsible opener in the space of a couple of weeks. He converted that new responsibility into an innings of 184 in the second Test at Lord's, batting for just over eight hours. Both in New Zealand and at Lord's the conditions called for steady concentration and tight defence, and Haynes made the adjustment like an old hand. It was not that he abandoned his strokes altogether, just that he was more selective about when to open the cupboard and use them. In the years to follow, he became better and better and his versatility is best realised through his record in both Test and one-day cricket. Greenidge was well established as one of the best batsmen in the game by the time Haynes arrived and the two developed into the consistent and high-class partnership that was an essential component in our long sequence of victories.

They were two entirely different personalities, Haynes full of life, always willing to talk and crack a joke, Greenidge quiet and withdrawn. I think the contrast helped their partnership as did the fact that they obviously had tremendous respect for each other's ability.

I first heard of Malcolm Marshall when I got back from Australia after the first season of WSC. Maurice Foster and one or two of the other Jamaican players reported they had been bowled out in a Shell Shield match in Barbados by 'a little boy' of whom we would soon be hearing a lot. The West Indies selectors appeared to share that view for they picked him for the official tour of India and Sri Lanka later that year on the evidence of that one performance. It was an inspired choice that gave Marshall an early introduction into international cricket.

The first time I actually saw Malcolm in action was in the nets during the 1979 World Cup in England. I couldn't believe this slim, unimposing young man was the new up-and-coming fast bowler I had been hearing about but I only needed to see him run up and bowl to appreciate what the selectors had seen in him. He had a very fast, rhythmical approach, left arm high up, close to the stumps and a smooth follow-through. He was under six feet tall and looked almost out of place alongside the other fast bowlers of the time, Roberts, Garner, Croft and myself, who were all over six feet tall. But even his lack of height proved an advantage in that he made the ball skid through. During the World Cup and on the tour of Australia and New Zealand, he was among the reserves but injuries to Roberts and Croft gave him his chance in three of the five Tests in England and he fitted in right from the start.

Malcolm went on to become the highest Test wicket-taker for the West Indies, a wonderful and deserved achievement. A lot of young fast bowlers come in like whirlwinds but quickly blow themselves out because they don't know about bowling. From the very beginning, he had excellent control and constantly thought about what he was doing. He would look at batsmen closely, spot their weakness and work on it. That habit, developed early, stood him in good stead. He was always a fierce competitor who was never satisfied unless he was taking wickets, which should be the attitude of any fast bowler worth his keep.

While these two young players were making their mark, it was to be the last series for Deryck Murray, who had given such great service as a player for all of seventeen years and whose role as deputy to Clive Lloyd, both on the field and during the turbulent times of the Packer crisis, was so important. Deryck was an efficient, rather than brilliant, keeper and a steady late-order batsman with a cool head who could be relied on in a crisis. He started as a twenty-year-old in England in 1963, when he kept wicket to Wes Hall, Charlie Griffith, Gary Sobers and Lance Gibbs. Now he was going out to an equally successful, if differently balanced attack.

It is always difficult to part with such valuable individuals but Deryck was thirty-seven and the wear and tear of so much cricket had obviously taken their toll. He was well below his best in England, missing several catches, and he was dropped for the tour of Pakistan a few months later. The decision was to have controversial consequences when we took on England at home early in 1981. As the selectors also omitted Andy Roberts from the Pakistan tour, with an explanation that he was being rested, the feeling in his native Trinidad was that Deryck was being rested too. However, David Murray, a Barbadian and no relation,

who had been second string for some time, took over
in Pakistan and had a very successful tour. He was a
high-class keeper, a small man with what they call in
the business 'a soft pair of hands' and a pretty fair batsman as well. He should have been brought in during the
England tour for he was the better keeper at that time.
Yet, when the team for the first Test against England
at the Queen's Park Oval in Trinidad was announced
and the Murray in it was David, not Deryck, all hell
broke loose.

As was almost inevitable in the West Indies, the
omission of a local favourite from the Test team was
seen as an insult to national honour and there was a
widespread campaign for a boycott of the Test. The
press and radio joined in and demonstrators paraded
outside the ground carrying placards to make their
point. It was not the first time Trinidadians have given
vent to their feelings at selection policies in this manner
– the fury at the dropping of Larry Gomes from the team
to England the previous summer was just as heated.

Trinidadians are by no means the only West Indians
who perceive discrimination and injustice when selection affects their own. To a greater or lesser extent,
the wrangle over Gomes and over Deryck Murray has
recurred in every territory in the West Indies. Even
board officials have criticised non-selection of their
island's players in West Indies teams and the first Test
against South Africa in April 1992 was spoiled by a
complete boycott of the match by fans in Barbados
largely, but by no means only because the local
favourite, fast bowler Andy Cummins, was left out.

I regret having to admit it but I fear such insularity
will continue. While we have played as a West Indies
team since our first tour of England in 1900, there is no
such entity as the West Indies, except in a very loose
geographical and historical sense. Repeated efforts to

have us come together in political union have failed and even the formation of an economic community, CARICOM, has been fragmented.

West Indies cricket, like our language, our systems of government and our education, was born out of British colonialism. But while almost all of the former colonies have become individual sovereign nations in the past thirty years, the West Indies team has retained its strong regional identity. Politicians pushing the integration theory are fond of using the cricket analogy to support their point.

Our collective performances and our many great individual players have brought a sense of pride and achievement to West Indian people as a whole and not only to those in the Caribbean. The hundreds of thousands who make their homes in England walk with a spring in their steps when the West Indies are on tour.

While it has been a great binding factor, it has also caused heated divisions, especially over team selection, since in almost every area of life, except cricket, we are separated by water. Each island identifies itself by its own distinctive landscape, accent, music, customs, even rum and beer.

I have heard serious arguments in cricket dressing-rooms over the relative merits of Jamaica's Appleton Rum and Barbados' Cockspur and Jamaica's Red Stripe beer and the Banks of Guyana and Barbados. Extend that attitude to cricket and you will take my point. How many demonstrators, I wonder, outside the Queen's Park Oval before that Test had ever seen David Murray keep wicket or watched Deryck's declining form in England?

Any team likes to know it has an advantage when playing at home but there have been times when we have been made to feel distinctly uncomfortable because the crowds in one country or another have not been happy with the selection. Clive Lloyd was booed in the nets and on his way to the wicket during that Trinidad Test. More recently, Richie Richardson was heckled even more viciously at Sabina Park in Jamaica because it was felt he was responsible for dropping Jeffrey Dujon, a Jamaican, out of the World Cup team and was rumoured to have made some uncomplimentary remarks about Jamaica. Once things are going well, our crowds can be fantastic and full of noisy support. That is not always the case and it is neither unusual nor surprising to hear some West Indian cricketers say they would rather play away from home because there isn't as much pressure on them.

The situation is compounded whenever India and Pakistan are touring since about half the populations of Trinidad and Guyana are of *East* Indian descent. They have retained strong cultural and religious ties with their mother countries and openly support their kith and kin. English players have told me they feel the same way when they play at The Oval in London where West Indians come in their thousands from the Brixton area to give us their backing.

So Deryck Murray, a soft-spoken, unassuming man, went out of West Indies cricket, to which he had given so much, in a welter of controversy he neither wanted nor deserved. It would surely have been better and less embarrassing to all concerned if the selectors had let him know the position and given him the option of announcing his retirement after the England tour, rather than being dropped after such a long time in the team.

CHAPTER 11

My Test place in jeopardy

The West Indies tour to Pakistan at the end of 1980 was my first to that part of the world. I had heard it was a tough place for fast bowlers, since the pitches were slow and usually prepared to assist spinners. By now Clive Lloyd had settled his pace policy and, even without Andy Roberts, who was being rested, we stuck to it. Sylvester Clarke, a big, strong Barbadian who had done well on the tour of India under Alvin Kallicharran a couple of years earlier, joined Colin Croft, Joel Garner, Malcolm Marshall and myself in the attack. This probably guaranteed that conditions would be even deader than usual and, as Pakistan had a powerful batting team with Javed Miandad, Majid Khan, Zaheer Abbas, Sadiq Mohammad and Wasim Raja, I anticipated plenty of bowling and stern opposition. We had an immediate hint of how tough things could be when we lost our first match against a very strong President's Eleven, for whom Miandad scored 130.

Any self-respecting cricketer wants to prove himself in all conditions and I was looking forward to the tour after the virtual washout in England. I never had the chance. In the very first one-day international at the National Stadium in Karachi, I bowled a ball to Mudassar Nazar which popped and he lobbed it straight into the air. I ran down the wicket, dived to take the catch and rolled over on my right shoulder, the one that had given so much trouble after the 1976 tour of England. The fall reactivated the injury so badly that I could hardly raise my right arm for a long time afterwards. With injections and other treatment, it got a little better as the tour went on and I never lost hope of playing in the later Tests but it was always no more than an outside chance. When I tried at practice, I could get no power in delivery and, even though I did play a three-day match just before the third Test and told myself I could make it, I knew in my heart I couldn't.

So it wasn't a very enjoyable tour for me personally. I was there to play cricket and instead spent most of my time just hanging around. The tour took in small towns that were packed into the itinerary for three-day matches, places such as Sukkur and Sahiwal, so I did see the country but accommodation and food outside the main cities were something of a culture-shock. In the cities, the hotels were of high international standard but in Karachi, where we least expected it, food poisoning hit three or four of us. Faoud Bacchus had it so bad that his face blew up like a football and you could hardly see his eyes.

The cricket, as we anticipated, was hard-fought, with scores low. We clinched the series 1–0 with a good win, by 156 runs, in the second Test at Faisalabad, had the better of the three drawn matches and won all three one-day internationals. Not many teams have beaten Pakistan at home but we were a very strong side while several of the Pakistanis, notably Zaheer, Majid and Sadiq, were past their best. Our success was again based equally on the superb batting of Richards and on the penetrative power of our fast bowling, even on such pitches. Richards batted as if he had played in Pakistan all his life, not as someone who had to adjust to the peculiar pitches. He scored an unbeaten 120 out of 249 in the final Test and, while he totalled 346 runs in the Tests, no-one else managed more than 150 for us.

The Pakistanis relied mainly on their spinners, Mohammed Nazir, the off-spinner, and Iqbal Qasim, the left-armer, who took 33 wickets between them, but our fast quartet proved what could be achieved by top-class bowling, no matter how adverse the conditions. Since his two most experienced bowlers, Roberts and myself, were absent, it simply strengthened Clive Lloyd's belief in his pace policy although Rangy Nanan, the Trinidadian off-spinner on his one and only tour, did play a definite part in the Test win at Faisalabad with two wickets in each innings.

With a deceptively short run-up, Clarke bowled as quickly as anyone, but his tour will be remembered more for an unfortunate incident in the last Test at Multan than for his bowling. Fielding on the third-man boundary, he was pelted with oranges, pebbles and other objects and was hit a number of times. It was not clear what caused the commotion but we had come to realise that was the way crowds there would amuse themselves! After twenty minutes or so, Clarke suddenly picked up a brick, used as a boundary marker, and tossed it into the stands where it struck a spectator who happened to be a local students' leader. The sight of him being stretchered out of the ground, blood streaming from a head wound, was enough to spark a riot but, somehow, the crowd was placated and a potentially ugly scene did not materialise. Alvin Kallicharran had the presence of mind to go on his knees in prayer which helped cool things, and we all breathed a sigh of relief when an operation saved the spectator's life.

I watched it all from the pavilion, nursing my injured shoulder, and it will always remain a regret that I never played Test cricket against Pakistan, having also missed the 1977 series in the Caribbean. They have players of enormous talent and produced one of the finest batsmen of the present generation, Javed Miandad, and one of the few genuine all-rounders of top quality, Imran Khan.

To see Miandad at the wicket, it would be hard to guess that he is a batsman fit to rank among the best of all time. Square-on in his stance and with plenty of bottom hand in his strokes, he does not conform to the textbook. Yet it is a technique that works for him and has made him one of the game's highest scorers, in Tests as well as one-day internationals. I played against him quite a bit in the one-dayers and he would have 40 or 50 runs on the board without anyone really noticing. He just accumulated his runs with neat placements and the occasional attacking shot off a loose ball. He picked up the ball so early in its flight that he would get himself into a comfortable position to play the shots he wanted. He has been the linchpin of their batting since the retirement of Majid, Zaheer and the Mohammads and one of the main reasons for their high standing in world cricket, now World Cup champions.

The other, even more fundamental reason, was Imran who, along with Ian Botham, Kapil Dev and Richard Hadlee, is one of only four cricketers of my time who could qualify as genuine all-rounders. There were one or two others who could bat and bowl but they were not in that class. Like all the great all-rounders, Imran was capable of turning a match with a single innings or one bowling spell.

He had enormous physical strength, fierce pride in his country and a strong belief in its cricketers. As a bowler he could generate extreme pace and used the crease cleverly to vary the angle of his delivery. As a batsman, he had a correct style, using a straight bat and plenty of common sense. Over and above his all-round capacity, Imran overcame the politics which always seemed to beset cricket in that part of the world, set the example himself on the field, and made his players believe in themselves. His influence was very similar to Clive Lloyd's on the West Indies.

After returning home from Pakistan, I went straight into the Shell Shield to prepare for the tour by England, concerned that my absence from Test cricket shouldn't be delayed any longer. Four days after arriving back, I was in the Jamaica team for the first match of the season against Trinidad and Tobago. The shoulder injury had all but cleared up by now and tablets provided by Dr Paul Wright, who had treated the original problem, hastened the complete recovery. I bowled nearly 28 overs against Trinidad and Tobago in the opening match and took five for 96; and had 22 overs, if only one wicket, in the second match against the Combined Islands in St Kitts with no ill effects.

By this time, Andy Roberts was back in action, refreshed after his rest from Pakistan and taking wickets by the bucketful, so I knew that competition for fast bowling places for the England series would be tight. My qualms that I would be the odd man out were confirmed when I learned, during our Shield match against Guyana, that I wasn't in the team for the first one-day international against England in St Vincent a few days later. Sylvester Clarke was, along with Roberts, Garner and Croft.

As it happened, the disciplinary committee of the West Indies Board was meeting on the brick-throwing incident at that same time and it was only after their decision to hand Clarke a three-match suspension that I was called in as a replacement. It might have been that the selectors were still unsure about my fitness but, had I not played in that one-day match, I would not have had the opportunity of reminding them that I was around.

Conscious of the situation, especially with Clive Lloyd on the opposing side, I really 'slipped myself' in the match against Guyana and I'm sure that that convinced the captain I was fully fit and ready to return – even though he collected an unbeaten century himself. By the time of the St Vincent one-day international, the first of the series, I was feeling fully confident of myself and, in a nail-biting finish, clean bowled the last two men, John Emburey and Chris Old, to give the West Indies victory by two runs. It was the first big match ever staged in St Vincent and it seemed as if the entire population of 80,000 turned out at the Arnos Vale ground, which nestled in between the airstrip and the Caribbean Sea. They saw an unforgettable, if low-scoring, match. We were bowled out for 127 and all seemed lost when England were 123 for eight but, with wild scenes around the ground, I got those last two wickets to snatch the victory.

My place in the team was again settled. But I'm not so sure it would have been had Clarke not thrown that brick in Pakistan.

CHAPTER 12

Reaching our peak

I was convinced when we came out of World Series
Cricket that this West Indies team had the potential to
be one of the strongest of all. It was a view supported
by the way it played in the World Cup in 1979 and in
Australia the following winter, 1979–80.

Our momentum was then upset by the disputes
in New Zealand and by the weather in England and
Pakistan that spoiled so much of the cricket. The British summer of 1980 had been so wet that we hardly
got through a day's play without interruption; in
Pakistan as well we lost something like three full days
in the last two Tests, both drawn. We won one Test in
each case but it would have been more had the rain
stayed away.

Our hopes for a full, uninterrupted series when
England came to the Caribbean early in 1981 were
again thwarted and we had to wait a bit longer before
we could start reeling off the kinds of results that
really confirmed our status. The Trinidad Test was
surrounded by the controversy over Deryck Murray's
omission and held up at the start by the sabotage of
the covers that left damp spots on the pitch and the
bowlers' run-up. The atmosphere wasn't particularly
pleasant but we won all the same, by an innings and
79 runs. The match brought me a personal landmark,
my 100th Test wicket when I had Brian Rose, the

Somerset left-hander, caught by David Murray in the second innings. Colin Croft also chalked up his 100th wicket later that day and we made our way to Guyana, happy to be already ahead in the series and free of the controversy of Trinidad.

When we were in Trinidad, we learned that Bob Willis, England's fast bowler and vice-captain, would have to return home because of a knee injury. By the time we got to Georgetown, Robin Jackman of Surrey had been summoned as a replacement, something of a surprise choice as he had never played for England and was thirty-five years of age. Our county players reported he was a typical English bowler with good control at fast-medium but nothing to give anyone sleepless nights. However when a Jamaican sports-caster, Ed Barnes, raised the issue of Jackman's South African contacts, the news filtered down the Caribbean to Georgetown and a dispute flared.

The Guyana government, headed by President Forbes Burnham, had always taken a strong stance against anyone with such contacts and had even threatened to ban Gary Sobers several years earlier after his trip to Ian Smith's Rhodesia. It had also stopped a few minor teams coming there because they included players who had been to South Africa, but no-one expected it to have such courage of its convictions as effectively to cancel a Test match by banning an England player. But it did.

Of course, it didn't happen as quickly and as finally as that – and not only the Guyana leg but the entire tour was involved. There were discussions and more discussions as we waited around the Pegasus Hotel in Georgetown for the decision, hearing a lot but not understanding much about a document called the Gleneagles Agreement. All the while, we were confined indoors by the pouring rain that would probably have washed out the Test in any case.

Not surprisingly, the Guyana government would not relent, Jackman had to leave, and the second Test was cancelled as England would not play without him. But the waiting didn't end there. Tests still had to be played in Barbados, Antigua and Jamaica and the individual governments needed to say yes or no to the tour continuing. In any other country, the situation would not have arisen because a single government would have given its verdict and that would have been that. In this case, three separate, independent governments were involved and it was quite feasible that two could have said yes and the other no. The feeling against white rule and apartheid in South Africa was always understandably strong in the West Indies but not all the governments were as intransigent in their attitude as Guyana's. Those deciding the future of this tour eventually came to the collective decision that Jackman be allowed entry and the tour continued.

It was not the first time that international cricket had become entwined in the long tentacles of the South African problem, nor was it to be the last. I have always taken a keen interest in the situation there and was not blind to the issues involved. I'm sure most of our players also appreciated it was a complex political matter that went beyond cricket but, as cricketers, we simply wanted a decision one way or the other. It was frustrating sitting around waiting for someone to tell us whether we still had a Test series or whether we could pack up and go home.

By the time we got started again with the third Test at Kensington Oval, I had not played for nearly a month and was raring to go. I didn't have to wait that long. We lost four early wickets after we were sent in, including Richards caught at slip off Graham Dilley for a duck, and only recovered to 265 all out through a tremendous century by Lloyd who had also checked a middle-order collapse in Trinidad and was batting better and better the older he got.

The people seemed to sense we had something special in store for them on the second day, the Saturday, and they were everywhere when we got to the ground, jam-packed into stands and even sitting on the roofs. It was typical Test match atmosphere, West Indies style, an excited buzz of anticipation that sets the adrenaline flowing. And we didn't disappoint the fans, bowling England out for 122. After that, Richards entertained them for the next two days with an unbeaten 182 that virtually settled the result as England could only manage 224 in their second innings after we had declared. The margin of victory was 298 runs.

Judging by the number of times I've been questioned about it ever since, most people seem to remember that Test for my first over to Geoff Boycott in England's first innings. If I haven't heard a hundred times that it was the fastest over ever, I haven't heard it once. Memory fades with time but, on seeing the video replay for the first time during England's 1990 Test in Barbados, I believe there were times I bowled faster, such as at The Oval in 1976. Geoff was alongside me in the Sky television commentary box when they put the video on the screen and, nine years on, he didn't enjoy it any more!

I was amused, but not surprised, to learn that he had spent the rest day of the Barbados Test playing over the first innings dismissal in his head and actually went to the local TV station in order to watch the video replay. Seymour Nurse, the former West Indies batsman who was the Barbados government coach, said he'd told Boycott he was surprised he could be bowled like that. 'It meant he wasn't behind the line of the ball,' Seymour pointed out. It was a correct assessment but it led to Boycott's second innings dismissal as well.

Perfectionist that he was, Boycott was intent on getting behind the ball second time round. As it turned out, I managed to get the fifth delivery of my opening over to lift sharply and, right in line, Geoff could only fend it off into Joel Garner's waiting hands at gully. When we saw the replay together nine years later when sharing the TV commentary on the same Kensington Oval ground, Geoff said he didn't mind getting out when he knew he did the right thing but he couldn't stand it when he knew he was technically at fault, as he had been in the first innings.

There was no cricketer of my time with a more single-minded commitment to his game. He studied batting as if he was doing a university thesis on it and never tired of practising to reach perfection. Touring the West Indies, he would always find someone to bowl to him in the nets after the other England players had packed it in for the day. A groundsman or a watching schoolboy, it didn't matter to Boycott as long as he was batting. It was as if he had a fixation about it and he valued nothing more highly than his wicket. He would pat back a half-volley or block a long-hop if he felt there was the slightest risk of getting out off it. I rarely tempted him to cut or to hook with something short and wide because I knew it was a waste of energy. He would just let it go by and I certainly can't recall him being out to an attacking stroke when I played against him. This made him a very difficult, and frustrating, man to bowl to because he also developed a very tight defensive technique.

Unlike some top batsmen, he also relished a challenge, was always ready to battle it out whatever the conditions. When I first played against him in the early 1980s, he was past his prime but he never lost his appetite for batting; and one of the last times I bowled to him was for Derbyshire against Yorkshire on a fast pitch with uneven bounce at Abbeydale Park in Sheffield. Everything was in my favour and my five wickets in the second innings included his. But he was the only one who got stuck in, scoring 69 out of 180. He came up to me in the bar afterwards and said it was one of the most enjoyable innings he had had for some time. Being Geoffrey Boycott, I knew he was absolutely serious.

As if the tour hadn't more than its fair share of trouble everyone was thrown into a state of shock and sadness when we got to the ground on the Sunday, the third morning of the Barbados Test, to learn of the sudden death at the team's hotel the night before of Ken Barrington, the former England batsman who was assistant manager of the team. Our personal relationship didn't go beyond a nod and a quiet 'how're things' when we saw each other in the hotel or at the ground, but I had grown up listening to enough Test cricket to have developed a healthy respect for the way he so often held up the West Indies during the 1960s when our bowling was so strong.

Cricket is a wonderful fraternity and the loss of one of its number, even if he's only been a name from some distant Test match, is always cause for sadness. Ken had been with us, seemingly hale and hearty, only the day before, fully involved with his team. The trauma was etched on the faces of the England players as we stood in silent tribute prior to the start of play and Kensington Oval, usually reverberating with excitement, was as quiet as a cathedral that day.

It was a tribute to England that they pulled themselves together to draw the last two Tests, even if with some help from the weather. It is possible that the carnival spirit in Antigua at the time went a long way towards lifting their gloom. It was the island's first Test match, played on the small, intimate Recreation Ground right in the heart of the capital, St John's, and that in itself was cause for joyful celebrations. The wedding of its most famous son, Viv Richards, two days earlier, was the icing on the cake, and it was obligatory that Viv should further glorify the occasion with a century and he inevitably did.

We had just come from Barbados where the crowds were ecstatic at our success but I've known nothing to quite match the excitement that gripped Antigua that week. For the island itself, and for the Leeward and Windward Islands as a whole, the staging of a Test ended a long struggle for proper recognition in West Indies cricket. For some reason I have never heard properly explained, it was not until 1966 that they were brought into the mainstream when they were included as a Combined team in the first Shell Shield tournament. Before that, they had been given only the odd first-class match, mainly against touring teams and, without exposure, they could get no-one into the Test side. In the twenty-five years since the breakthrough, they have certainly made up for lost time. They won the Shell Shield in 1981, after which they split into separate teams, and the Leewards, the 1990 Red Stripe Cup champions, have taken more places in the Test eleven in recent years than any other territory.

Viv Richards and Andy Roberts, both Antiguans, were their first truly great players. Their countrymen proudly and rightfully lived in the reflected glory of their triumphs and those of their modern successors such as Richie Richardson and Curtly Ambrose. The island of Antigua is just over one hundred square miles with a population of about 80,000, but Richards and Roberts brought it international recognition in at least one sphere of activity and are revered as national heroes. When Viv hit his hundred in that match, I am sure the people would have readily proclaimed him King. Come to think of it, he has long since been that, even if unofficially.

The Recreation Ground quickly established itself as one of the best batting pitches in the Caribbean and, in that inaugural Test, England had no difficulty holding on for a draw. It is a fair indication of its character that I made what was then my highest Test score, 58, in that match and bettered it five years later in the same place, with 73, also against England.

We led by 187 on first innings in Antigua but, with the match reduced to four days by rain, could not turn that advantage into victory. The pattern in the final Test in Jamaica was similar. The lead was 157 and the rain again prevented us making the most of it. Yet, even as they struggled, England had some reason for optimism with Graham Gooch's 153 in the first innings and David Gower's unbeaten 154 in the second. They are two high-class players who were to carry England's batting through the decade of the 1980s and into the 1990s.

CHAPTER 13

Turning pro

No sooner was the final Test of the 1981 home series over than I was off again for England in my new occupation as a full-time professional cricketer, to join Rishton in the Lancashire League. The northern leagues had provided a long line of West Indian cricketers not only with their first professional contracts but with their first taste of English conditions as well; but, for me, the cricket was a big disappointment.

It was a particularly wet season, especially in the north. The standard of play was low, and it presented no challenge. Rishton did have covers but they seldom did the job and, when we played out, it always seemed to be wet even if the weather had been dry all week. I played on only one dry pitch all summer on which I took eight wickets for next to nothing and caused another batsman to retire hurt.

The people of Rishton and at the club were tremendous. There was plenty of excitement after I was signed and our wicketkeeper, the butcher, Frank, was the centre of attention prior to the season. Asked how he was going to take the thunderbolts from the new signing, he replied that he was in the right job. He would insert a couple of steaks in his gloves! The fans were exceedingly loyal to the club, which was the focal social point of the town, and I don't think we would ever have started play without the most ardent fan of the lot, a lady I only remember as Betty, whose pointed comments every weekend could be heard right across the ground.

As with most of the teams in the leagues, there was a local 'derby'. Ours involved East Lancashire, the team from Blackburn, Rishton's big neighbour. As it happened, I was injured during the match but it was ruined by rain in any case. At the end of the season I had taken 86 wickets, which put me second in the League's bowling averages, and I also managed to score a few runs. I was told that crowds also increased significantly. I made lasting friends with many of the people of Rishton and the chairman, Mr Woodhouse, and the team captain, both came to Jamaica to stay with my parents soon afterwards. But the cricket was not what I was looking for at that stage of my career.

Luckily, an offer from Clive Lloyd gave me the chance simultaneously to experience county cricket for the first time. Since Rishton's matches were only at weekends, I had plenty of free time and Clive suggested I play mid-week and, where possible, Sunday League matches for Lancashire which he was captaining for the first time. Quite apart from cricket at a more competitive level, his invitation also allowed me to test the water of the county scene so that, when Derbyshire offered me a contract two years later, I knew what I was getting into.

My time with Lancashire included one of the most exciting matches I've ever played in, the semi-final of the 1981 NatWest Trophy one-day tournament against Northamptonshire at Northampton. I was looking forward to a Lord's final and reckoned I was on my way when we took Northants' ninth wicket 13 runs short of their target. As Jim Griffiths came in, a couple of our players informed me he was the world's worst batsman, the type who was batting no. 11 only because there was no no. 12. That might have been so but, that day, he held on with Tim Lamb, Northants got the runs and I had to wait some years for my trip to Lord's for that final.

The next item on my agenda was another tour of Australia that winter, the fifth time I was returning in the seven years since my first trip there. It was again a series of three Tests as we shared the season with Pakistan. It might have been short but it was as competitively contested and as enjoyable as any I have ever been in. Defeat in a close, low-scoring first Test at the Melbourne Cricket Ground immediately put us under pressure since we had only two more to pull back, not four as in a full series. The pitch at the MCG was sub-standard and contributed to the result but those at Sydney and Adelaide favoured batting and we had to fight like the devil each time to bowl Australia out twice. We failed to make an impression at the SCG even though we had more than a day available in their second innings. With time taken out for bad light, Australia held out comfortably with only four wickets down for 200 thanks to a dogged, unbeaten 127 by John Dyson. It meant we had to win at Adelaide to share the series and keep the Frank Worrell Trophy.

It proved one of the best Tests I've ever played in. It swung from one side to the other from beginning to end until what could truly be termed a captain's innings from Clive Lloyd won it for us by five wickets with three of the mandatory final twenty overs remaining.

There is no ground in the world like the MCG and no more patriotic crowd. It is a huge concrete centre that can hold 100,000 and has easily the biggest outfield in the game. In my experience, it also had a pitch often uneven in bounce and pace. This guarantees excitement for the spectator with wickets falling and the probability of an outright result but the quality of the cricket itself suffers. In that 1981–82 Test, even with batsmen like Greg Chappell, Allan Border and Kim Hughes on their side and Viv Richards, Clive Lloyd and Desmond Haynes on ours, the highest total in the match was 222. Hughes threw his bat at everything and rode his luck for a dazzling, unbeaten 100 on the first day that was probably the turning point of the match after Australia were 8 for three wickets. For the crowd, the highlight was Dennis Lillee's history-making performance as he passed Lance Gibbs' Test record of 309 wickets when he had Larry Gomes caught at second slip by Greg Chappell on the second day. It was an emotional occasion marked by the waving of Australian flags and the playing of 'Waltzing Matilda' on the PA system. Even that could not compare with the sheer bedlam of the previous afternoon when we lost four wickets for 10 runs in reply to their 198, three to Lillee. To hear the crowd of 40,000 chanting 'Lill-ee, Lill-ee, Lill-ee' as he steamed in was enough to make the hair rise on the back of the neck and do funny things to the insides of batsmen. When he bowled Viv Richards for 2 with the last ball of the day, the whole place erupted. I have never heard such noise on any ground anywhere.

Lillee finished the innings with seven for 83 and the match with 10 for 127. It was the last series he would play against the West Indies as he retired a couple of years later with 355 Test wickets, then the record. We had first come across him in the 1975–76 series when he and Jeff Thomson did so much damage, but while Thomson faded after a shoulder injury, Lillee's standard never dropped.

He had almost everything you could ask for in a fast bowler, strength, stamina, a well-balanced run, a flowing action and good pace. He also had intelligence, aggression and courage and used every trick in the book to try and get batsmen out. He made mental notes on every player and knew who was susceptible to the bouncer, who was weak against his outswinger and who was vulnerable to his brand of psychological warfare. His bold fight to overcome a serious back injury that could have ended his career early says a lot about his character and he was nothing less than a national hero in Australia. As fellow fast bowlers, we often chatted about our craft, especially during the Packer years, and I learned a lot about technique and attitude from watching and listening to Dennis Lillee.

Our loss in the first Test and draw in the second of that series meant we had to win at Adelaide. No ground contrasts with the MCG more than the Adelaide Oval, with its old wooden stands and pavilion on the square boundary, its open terracing and its squeezed, oblong shape with elongated straight boundaries and tight square ones. The difference extended to the pitch which was invariably flat and true with just a little bit to encourage the bowlers. While less than 800 runs were scored at the MCG, over 1,200 were made at Adelaide.

Our victory was a wonderful way to finish a memorable season and underlined the fighting spirit we had so frequently been told West Indian cricketers lacked once the chips were down. Our record spoke for itself but, after both the first Test in Melbourne and the second in Sydney, we kept hearing and reading that we couldn't stand up to pressure. We needed 220 to win at Melbourne and fell for 161. Then we couldn't bowl Australia out in plenty of time in Sydney.

Now the same taunt was being thrown at us again as Australia, in spite of a first-innings deficit of 151, started the final day comfortable at 341 for four. They were 190 ahead and apparently so confident of drawing the match that several bottles of champagne had

been moved into the dressing-room coolers in anticipation of regaining the Frank Worrell Trophy. A few
years earlier, they also had the champagne on ice in
the final of Packer's World Series Cup at the Sydney
Showground only to be disappointed. Their confidence
again proved premature.

We came out that last day absolutely determined
to win and played some inspired cricket. Two tremendous catches set the example, one by Desmond
Haynes at short extra-cover to account for Rod Marsh
off me and the other, a real blinder at short-leg, by
Faoud Bacchus off Joel Garner to dismiss Kim Hughes
for 84. Bacchus was as good an all-round fielder as I've
seen and a good-looking batsman who just lacked the
concentration to make the highest level. Those two
catches set off an Australian collapse in which the
last six wickets fell for 24 in just over an hour and put
us in with a real chance. Our target was 236 and, even
though anything approaching 250 to win in under a day
is bound to be tough, our breakthrough had given us a
big boost. In addition, the pitch was still in good order
and Greenidge and Richards, neither of whom was at
his best on the tour, added 100 for the second wicket
to get us off to a solid start. But then they went within
a few runs of each other and it was left to Lloyd to
carry his team home with a masterful display. As we
counted down the target in the dressing-room, run by
run, some of us couldn't bear to look until Clive finally hit the winning runs, finishing unbeaten on 77. Joel
Garner, Colin Croft and myself, overcome with joy after
an emotionally-draining match, immediately ran on to
the field to hoist the captain to our shoulders and carry
him back to the pavilion in triumph.

After the Adelaide Test of the previous tour two
years earlier, most cricket writers predicted it would be
Clive's last Test in Australia. They said much the same

thing this time. He was, after all, in his thirty-eighth year and his knees were not in pristine condition. Yet he was batting and catching at slip as well as ever and had become a confident, positive and respected captain. He still had a lot of cricket left in him and I believe he was not yet satisfied that the team he had moulded was playing to its full potential.

There were two major individual advances on the Australian tour. Larry Gomes finally established himself in the Test side with centuries at Sydney and Adelaide, and Jeffrey Dujon showed himself to be a batsman with a special flair. When David Murray had to miss the final Test with a broken finger, Dujon came in as a capable and agile wicketkeeper, well suited to coping with the balance of our attack. Both Dujon and Gomes were to figure prominently in the unrivalled record of the next three years when the West Indies did not lose a single Test until beaten by Australia in the final Test of the next series there in 1984–85.

Larry came in at an opportune time, just when Alvin Kallicharran was on his way out, and filled very much the same role in the middle order. Larry was neat and slim, almost anonymous. He stroked and caressed the ball and added variety to the order since he was a left-hander who forced the bowlers to adjust their line. While most West Indians delight in playing all the shots and hitting the ball as hard as possible, Larry devised a very effective method to suit himself. He perfected certain strokes and denied himself those he felt would get him out. He never wore a helmet and never hooked. But he had a nice sense of timing, using the pace of the ball to nudge and push for runs. And he had an unflappable temperament that brought the best out of him in a crisis. For many years he was the unsung hero of the team, his value glossed over because he was overshadowed by the likes of Richards,

Greenidge and Lloyd, big men who were so flamboyant and powerful. Within our dressing-room, there was tremendous respect for this soft-spoken Trinidadian and his consistent contribution to our successes.

The 1981–82 Australian tour was also outstanding for me personally. Even though I had a few problems with a dodgy cartilage in my left knee, I never bowled faster, or better, than in those three-and-a-half months. As I look back at the statistics, they support my assessment – 24 wickets in the three Tests, including eleven at Melbourne, at an average of only 14. Throughout, I sensed everything was just flowing. There was no little jerk or hesitation in run-up or delivery which can upset rhythm and reduce pace, no matter how hard you try. I didn't feel after releasing the ball that I'd really expended any energy and it was just a matter of getting back to my mark to move in again. There were other times when I was striving for pace so hard that I would feel I'd lost another pound of strength with every ball I bowled, but there was nothing like that here. I was always eager to bowl and confident I'd get wickets.

There was one particular World Series Cup match against Australia at the WACA ground in Perth when I knew in myself I was bowling as quick as I had ever done. This was where I had got my first Test wicket and, with its pace and bounce, I always looked forward to bowling there. On that day, I was really firing, especially in one over in which I bowled Rick Darling with one ball and had Greg Chappell with the next, caught by Haynes at short leg off one that kicked sharply. I probably maintained pace for longer periods at The Oval in 1976 but, for a short burst, I would have to put that down as my fastest.

A week later, I managed to find another 'special' first ball to Greg Chappell that he edged to Murray. It was one of seven ducks for the Australian captain for the season and three of them were first ballers against us. It just goes to prove that even great players go through bad patches – and Greg Chappell was a great player as he had proved over and over before that. I first came across him and his brother, Ian, on my first-class debut for Jamaica against the 1973 Australians and Greg collected a century. They were quite different batsmen and quite different characters. Greg, tall and correct, did things in the orthodox manner. He would play straight into the 'V' and ignore any crossbatted shots until he was in for some time and seeing the ball well. He didn't take the chances Ian did and stuck to the book in his selection of strokes although he had most of them. Once he got in, it was very hard to prise him out but, in that series, he was a marked man as Australia's best batsman and captain and he cracked under the pressure. Somehow, I don't think we could have undermined Ian's confidence in the same way. He was one of the toughest cricketers I've come across.

For all my successes – or, who knows, it might have been because of them – I was increasingly bothered by a painful left knee. I needed to have it heavily strapped before taking the field and was occasionally forced to reduce my run-up. The problem was diagnosed as the lateral cartilage and, at the end of the tour, Dr Merv Cross operated on it in a Sydney hospital. He reported afterwards that it was 100 per cent successful but, while there were no complications, it did take a lot of weight training and physiotherapy to regain mobility. It was seven months before I was playing again, but I soon came to appreciate that the knee would never be quite as strong and that I would never bowl really fast after that.

Within a year, I had cut my run down and adjusted my style.

CHAPTER 14

Off the short run

Seven months is a long time for a fast bowler to be laid up waiting for an injury to heal. As, back in Jamaica, I worked with gym exercises and jogging to build back my knee after the cartilage operation in Sydney early in 1982, my mind was on the new ground I'd be breaking on my return.

While in Australia, I had been approached by Jack Simmons, the Lancashire player, to join Tasmania for the 1982–83 season. Jack spent many winters with the island-state and had worked hard to bring them into the Sheffield Shield competition. After a few years on an experimental basis, they were being given full status and he was keen to have a couple of experienced overseas players to boost them. Not only was it a challenge but it meant returning to Australia and I didn't take long to accept the contract.

At the time, I couldn't have known I would have to start after a lengthy lay-off following a cartilage operation. I was a little nervous as to how I would go, especially since there were such great expectations in Tasmania. I needn't have worried. Our first match was against New South Wales at the SCG and, within my first two overs, I clean bowled Ian Davis and had Rick McCosker lbw, both Test players. It was 23 October and my first match at any level since the first Test at the Adelaide Oval in early February. My relief and elation were understandable, especially as Tasmania completed a famous victory by seven wickets.

It was the only season I spent with the island-state. Even so, I could not fully complete it as I had to return to Jamaica to play an obligatory Shell Shield match in order to qualify for the home series against India. Sheffield Shield cricket was of a high standard and extremely competitive. The Tasmanian team was bubbling with enthusiasm and, in David Boon and Stuart Saunders, had two very talented young cricketers. Boon has gone on to be an important member of the Australian Test side but I'm disappointed the same is not true of Saunders who had natural all-round ability as a leg-spinner and batsman. I suspect he didn't have the temperament to match, the downfall of so many young cricketers.

The stint with Tasmania was also a chance to prove that my knee was back in working order and I bowled 371 overs for a return of 36 wickets without any adverse reaction. But I was always aware that it could not bear the strain it used to and knew in my heart of hearts that I would have to alter my run-up as so many fast bowlers had to do because of similar injuries. It was easier said than done, and it was Andy Roberts who gave me the inspiration, encouragement and advice that finally convinced me to do it.

Quite apart from our fellowship as fast bowlers in the West Indies team, Andy and myself were great personal friends from the time we first met while sharing twelfth-man duties, myself for Jamaica, he for the Combined Islands in a Shell Shield match at Sabina Park back in the early 1970s. We sat on the famous green bench in the Kingston Club pavilion that accommodated the players and chatted, mainly about cricket. Through our many tours together, I got to know and appreciate Andy even better, as a friend and as a cricketer. Because he was so quiet and unassuming, a lot of people formed the mistaken impression that he was unapproachable and moody. He certainly wasn't the type to go out and seek new friends but he was sincere. As a cricketer, he thought deeply about the game and was expert at reading its various complexities.

I benefited over and over from his advice, as early as my first Test wicket. Just sitting around in the hotel room together talking, I learned a lot from him about bowling and, every now and again, he would come up to me in the field and throw out a suggestion or a hint about how to deal with a particular batsman. More often than not, it would work.

We were two completely different bowlers with completely different actions. He was stronger physically and put his strength to full use in his bustling run-up and explosive delivery. After being one of the fastest bowlers in the game in his heyday, he skilfully modified his style and became a master of change of pace, even including two separate bouncers in his repertoire, one slower than the other.

In the 1983 home series against India he was thirty-two and some people seemed to regard him as 'over the hill'. Their comments were based on his reduction in pace more than anything else, but Andy never bothered with what people said. He just got on with the job and, in that series, led our bowling with 24 wickets, not so much through speed and hostility but with variation and movement. It was the way I would have to go as well although it took some time for me to make the change – under Andy's influence.

On my first tour of India the following year, I was still coming off my long run when Andy noticed I was tentative in putting my left foot down during the first Test at Kanpur in October 1983. He himself was nursing an injury at the time and not playing but, even from the pavilion, nothing escaped his eye. He was right, of course, because I was still not fully confident of my left knee. He suggested I get over it simply by cutting down my run, an option I was reluctant to accept. I didn't want anyone to feel I was slacking because of the operation but Andy told me not to be stupid. It was to my benefit and, therefore, to the team's. So I explained the situation to Clive Lloyd, got his approval and, with a few exceptions, operated off a reduced approach for the remainder of my career. There was the negative, if natural, initial reaction of trying something new. My run-up was second nature to me, much like a batsman's stance, and I was worried at first about the consequences of such a drastic alteration. In fact, I was pounding the knee down just as hard from the shorter run, which demanded the use of more body, and it really was a matter of overcoming the mental block.

My long run was something of a trademark and not everyone was happy that I abandoned it. I've had a couple of nicknames which tickled the fancy of the press and I'm not too sure who coined them but now they would have to go out the window. The image of a fast bowler isn't quite as macho when he's coming in off fifteen paces! One of those nicknames was 'Whispering Death' which I first heard from Paul Weaver, an English journalist, in the nets during the 1983 World Cup. Paul said the England boys apparently picked it up from Dickie Bird, the umpire who always had such a good rapport with the players. Dickie said I was the one fast bowler whose approach he couldn't detect by the morse-code of pounding footsteps since I was lighter on my feet than the others. That was where the 'whispering' part came in. 'Death' I wasn't too happy with. Geoff Boycott used the flattering phrase 'the Rolls-Royce of fast bowlers' after that 1981 opening over in Barbados but there were occasions when batsmen mouthed less complimentary words.

It wasn't until we got to Barbados for the 1984 Test against Australia that crowds back home were to see Holding Mark II and their reaction was most interesting. Barbadians had vivid recollections of the over to Boycott in 1981 and, when I came on first change and put my marker down, I could hear a murmur around the ground. They like their fast bowlers fast and, as far as they were concerned, fast bowlers take long run-ups. They lost no time in letting me know they weren't happy with the change they were seeing. 'Hey, Holding, give the ball more air,' I heard one man shouting. 'Pitch taking turn yet, Holding?' was another audible comment. They certainly rubbed it in but I had the last laugh. I had long since adapted to the style and, with the pitch wearing, the ball moved off the seam the last day. Malcolm Marshall and myself bowled out Australia for 97 in their second innings, leaving Greenidge and Haynes to knock off 21 runs for victory by ten wickets. As I came off, with four wickets to my name, I was feeling pretty pleased that I'd proved my point to a critical crowd. But I'm not sure if they appreciated it.

Very rarely did I revert to the long run after that. When I did so on a whim in my final Test in England at the Oval in 1984, it had an immediate effect. Going back out after tea on the fourth afternoon, I recognised a face in the crowd on the steps that led down from the old dressing-rooms, through the pavilion and on to the field. It belonged to a Surrey member with whom I'd chatted following the 1976 Test when I took my 14 wickets. As I passed, he said simply: 'Remember 1976'. He may have been just trying to jog my memory about our previous meeting but, as he said it, the thought occurred to me to briefly wind the clock back to 1976 and try the long run again. It was almost three years since I'd used it consistently and Clive Lloyd told me afterwards he thought I'd forgotten something in the dressing-room and was going back to fetch it as I was marking out my run.

I only kept it going for a few overs but, in that time, I broke a stubborn second-wicket stand by having Chris Broad caught at gully, followed by Allan Lamb, to a catch by Desmond Haynes at short-leg, and David Gower lbw. They all fell in the space of seventeen balls for five runs and, next day, the press made a big thing about my reversion to the long run. As wicketkeeper Jeffrey Dujon will attest, I was bowling no faster than off the shorter approach but, like so much in cricket, psychology played a big part.

When we came off, I sought out my friend on the steps and we had a beer together. But I didn't have the heart to tell him it was probably his idea that cost England three good wickets that day.

CHAPTER 15

The South African problem

I was in Tasmania in early January 1983 when the cricket world was shocked by the news that a team of West Indians had signed contracts to play in South Africa for the following two seasons in defiance of the United Nations sporting boycott, their own governments, and the West Indies Board. The South Africans had already shown their hand by dishing out vast sums of money to breach their international isolation and, in spite of the ban from Test cricket of those who went, had secured several leading England players and a somewhat more obscure group of Sri Lankans as their touring teams over the two previous years.

It should have been obvious that their next prized prey would be a West Indies team. It would be wonderful propaganda value in their campaign to prove to the world that their sport was racially integrated and that the horrible reality of apartheid was, somehow, exaggerated. They had been successful for some time in luring the odd West Indian to play in their provincial cricket but it was a remarkable coup to find as many as eighteen to make up the complete touring squad. Naturally, it was the one topic of cricket conversation wherever I went in Australia. The Australians, I sensed, recognised that their turn was next.

The feeling was that while most English and Australian players would feel no moral obligation against going to South Africa, it was astonishing that black West Indians could demean themselves by touring a country that practised racial discrimination by law and where, as it came to light, they had to be accorded 'honorary white' status. That, in effect, meant they were denouncing their race and their colour to become, even if only in name, something they were not. If it was an 'honour' to be white, then they must have felt it was a dishonour to be black.

I was deeply hurt and felt a strong sense of betrayal and even anger. Here was the whole world uniting in opposition to a system that dehumanised black people specifically because they were black and a group of black people were breaching that unity. All were fellow West Indians with whom I had played. I counted many as friends. It was not easy to take and when a British Sunday newspaper rang me in Hobart to ask my views, I could not hide my feelings. 'These men are selling themselves,' I told the reporter. 'If they were offered enough money they would probably agree to wear chains. They would do anything for money.'

Yet I was not entirely surprised. Money was, indeed, the crux of the matter. I had listened to discussions among the Jamaican team at the Silver Beach Hotel in Barbados in 1982 when the England rebel team under Graham Gooch and Geoff Boycott first stirred the hornet's nest and heard several players admit they would go anywhere for the sort of money being quoted. I noted that five of the Jamaicans in the team to South Africa – Lawrence Rowe, who was captain, Richard Austin, Herbert Chang, Everton Mattis and Ray Wynter – were at the Silver Beach that day and that seven Barbadians – Alvin Greenidge, Emmerson Trotman, Collis King, Franklyn Stephenson, Ezra Moseley, Sylvester Clarke and Albert Padmore – played in that Shell Shield match. Gregory Armstrong, the former Barbados fast bowler

who was one of the prime movers behind the South
Africa operation, was a regular visitor to the hotel and
to the dressing-rooms during that period, so it is not
being far-fetched to suggest the seed was then being
sown.

I voiced my opinion about South Africa loud and
clear at the time so that Armstrong knew where I
stood. I was taken aback, therefore, when I got a call
in the middle of the night in Hobart from Armstrong
and Rowe nearing the end of their tour asking if I
would be interested in a contract to play the last
two one-day matches against South Africa for them
on my way home from Australia. I had a long chat
with Rowe who did his best to gloss over the situation but he was simply naive. I told him that, by
being there, he was supporting apartheid and letting
his people down. It was something I could never
do for any amount of money, I said. 'How about
US$250,000 for the two matches?' Armstrong piped
in. 'Not for any amount of money,' I replied. And that
was the last I heard from anyone associated with that
tour.

However, I was repeatedly approached in the coming years on an unofficial basis by agents for the South
African cricket authorities who continued to test the
water. Following my retirement from Test cricket in
1987, the interest was even greater. Now that I wasn't
jeopardising my Test career, surely there was no hin-
drance, one South African county player told me. He
didn't understand my moral stance on the issue and I
didn't really expect him to.

Armstrong might have been bluffing when he made
his offer of what was an enormous amount of money. I don't know. I do know that all the players
did receive very sizeable contracts. The most reli-
able figure I have heard was US$100,000 for the two

seasons. I was certain where I stood and was disappointed that any West Indian should have accepted. But I appreciated that when people such as those who went were tempted with these sorts of figures, it could not have been easy to refuse. The majority were from poor and humble backgrounds and would have looked at it as immediately securing their futures.

Even with that proviso, I do not believe the Jamaicans either thought of the long-term repercussions or were properly advised. I can only speak about Jamaica because I know the situation was different in some of the other territories. Jamaicans have always taken a deep and conscious interest in the issue of South Africa and apartheid. The government, regardless of the party that holds it at the time, has been consistently strong in opposition, our international reggae artists such as Bob Marley and Peter Tosh were in the forefront of the struggle, and the media keeps the public well informed. So the Jamaicans should have known that their lives would change completely once they chose to go to South Africa. They would not be able to get any jobs, could play no cricket at any level and would have few friends left. That did not apply in Barbados where there was far more sympathy for the players' position but it certainly proved to be the case in Jamaica.

Unfortunately the rebel Jamaicans did not seem to think further than the mandatory West Indies Cricket Board ban that put them out of Test and regional cricket forever. Life turned out to be hell for those who remained at home. Rowe, a national hero when he started his Test career with a double century and a single century on debut in 1972, and followed with a triple against England in 1974, moved out to Miami. Wynter and Mattis also emigrated to the United States but Austin and Chang stayed in Jamaica and became broken men, psychologically scarred, jobless, penniless and friendless.

Mattis, a tall, stylish right-handed batsman, came from a large family in a depressed area of the middleclass community of Kingston, Barbican. His prowess on the cricket field made him a revered favourite son and, when he first played for the West Indies against England in 1981, the people of Barbican arranged for a truck to pick him up at the airport and proudly parade him around the area. They refused to let him go in the team bus because he had to go with his 'brethren', his Rastafarian friends to whom he had become a symbol of what could be achieved in spite of his roots. By going to South Africa, he shattered that image and shamed his former friends, most of whom refused even to talk to him.

None of those who joined Rowe's rebels could say they had a definite future in Test cricket. Many had either come or were coming to the end of their days in the Test team, such as Rowe himself, Alvin Kallicharran and Bernard Julien. Colin Croft was bothered by a bad back and the others, with the possible exception of David Murray and the fast bowler, Sylvester Clarke, were either on the fringes or simply useful Shell Shield players.

Two names that were being bandied about at the time did shock me, those of Desmond Haynes and Malcolm Marshall.

They were both playing club cricket in Australia, in Melbourne, and I had it on good authority in Tasmania that they had signed to go and that tickets had arrived for them. I just couldn't understand how two such promising young cricketers with so much ahead of them in West Indies cricket could have opted to join Rowe's renegades. Luckily, both for them and the game, they changed their minds, as Desmond revealed, after discussions with an Australian lawyer. How much poorer cricket would have been had they stuck to their original decision.

For the next eight years, the South Africans continued to disrupt world cricket. They predictably hit at Australia as they got Kim Hughes and his team to follow the Englishmen, Sri Lankans and West Indians for a couple of seasons. Each country dealt with its defaulting players separately so that England stipulated a three-year ban from Test cricket, Australia two years, Sri Lanka twenty-five years, and the West Indies life. England were again forced to bypass Guyana on their 1986 West Indies tour as the government refused to accept their players with South African connections and their 1988–89 tour of India was called off entirely when Graham Gooch, who led the rebel team to South Africa a few years earlier, was named captain.

It was time for the International Cricket Council (ICC) to take some unified stand to end the confusion and it came out with its resolution early in 1989. It was obviously a compromise and I saw nothing wrong with wiping the slate clean and starting from scratch so that every country had a specific understanding of the position. But the South Africans quickly assembled an England team under Mike Gatting, dramatically making their point that no amount of ICC legislation can stop cricketers going anywhere once the money is right.

At least the ICC penalties had been standardised.

Personally, I objected to any West Indian who had been to South Africa being allowed to play for the West Indies again. This is not to say I did not accept the necessity for the ICC ruling, and I had nothing against them playing in the Red Stripe Cup for those individual territories who wanted to include them. Jamaicans who went were not allowed to play for Jamaica because people did not want them and I felt the same thing should have held good for the West Indies team. If you represent the West Indies, you represent everybody in the Caribbean and a lot of people in the Caribbean don't want people like that representing them. I am one of them.

Things have changed significantly in the last couple of years in South Africa and everyone who wants to see that tortured country get over its problems and become truly democratic must be pleased with the developments. With the blessing of Nelson Mandela and the African National Congress (ANC), it has meant the return of South Africa to international cricket, their participation in the World Cup and their brief tour of the West Indies for their inaugural Test in April 1992. Similarly, they have been taken back by the Olympic movement and almost every other international sporting body.

Personally, I still have reservations about the haste with which everything was done to get them back, with no conditions at all. I may be unduly pessimistic but I am not satisfied that the dismantling of apartheid and the white government's move to democracy are irreversible and feel the cricket world should have waited a little longer before giving its stamp of approval. It didn't ring true with me that the South Africans should have been welcomed back into world sport as quickly as they were, almost like long lost brothers. The entire World Cup schedule was even revised to accommodate them, and the West Indies Board, always so meticulous in its pre-planning, agreed in only a few days to slot them in for their brief tour. Money seems to be talking just as loudly now as it was when they were paying out fat cheques to lure rebel teams.

I don't say categorically that I wouldn't go if given the chance now that things are changing. But I would want to talk to people on both sides of the racial and political divide and to hear first-hand from the people themselves what they feel of the current situation. I do believe, however, that sport can be the catalyst to improve racial relations in South Africa as it was in the West Indies. Young sportsmen playing with and against each other learn to admire and respect each other's ability. I earnestly hope it is not too long before a democratically elected government, representative of all the people, is in place in South Africa and that all its people can play normal sport in a normal society.

CHAPTER 16

Dealing with disappointment

Disappointment is an unwanted yet frequent companion of all sportsmen and we all walk hand in hand with it at some time during our careers. I certainly came to know it well several times but never as intimately as in the World Cup final of 1983.

The West Indies won the Cup in 1975 and retained it in 1979 without losing a match in either tournament. We were firm favourites to complete the hat-trick. It was widely considered a mere formality since we had not only won the first two tournaments but also the three-way World Series Cup in Australia whenever we were involved. Also we had just come from a home series in early 1983 against India in which we were never pressed in either the Tests, winning 2–0, or the one-day internationals, winning 3–1.

The strength and balance of our side was not seriously affected by the exodus to South Africa since the one player I feared we would miss, the wicketkeeper David Murray, had been adequately replaced by Jeffrey Dujon.

What many people overlooked, including many of our players, was the unpredictability of the one-day game. This was immediately evident in our first match at Old Trafford. We played badly and lost by 34 runs against the same Indian team we had beaten so easily a couple of months earlier in the Caribbean. The Indians had a very modest one-day record and did not get past the first round of the two previous World Cup tournaments but they completely outplayed us. They batted consistently to total 262 for eight off their 60 overs and took advantage of our careless batting against their mainly medium-pace attack to have us 157 for nine before Andy Roberts and Joel Garner saved some of our embarrassment with a last-wicket stand of 71. We put that behind us as a one-off and romped through to the final without any further complications, including a second round victory by 66 runs over India at The Oval in which Viv Richards made 119.

Perhaps we should have paid a little more attention to how India reached the Lord's final in the first place. They not only defeated us in that opening match but went on to qualify for the semi-finals with a crushing win by 118 runs over Australia in the second round. They then swept past England by six wickets in the semi-final to set up their appointment with destiny.

We could hardly have made a better start to the final. The weather was grey and overcast in the morning, we had the advantage of bowling first on winning the toss and Roberts quickly removed India's most dangerous batsman, Sunil Gavaskar, who edged an outswinger to Dujon with only two runs scored. They never picked up after that and were all out for 183. This should not have been a total to tax a good batting side over 60 overs, especially as the weather had turned bright and sunny. Pakistan had mustered 184 for eight in our semi-final which we knocked off for the loss of two wickets, and even when Australia piled up 273 for six in beautiful batting conditions at Lord's in an earlier match, we lost only three wickets in making them. So victory now was treated as a foregone conclusion and each batsman seemed to go out with the attitude that if he didn't get the runs, someone after him would. They played a lot of airy-fairy shots, trying to get the runs in quick time instead of just batting normally until the Cup was secured. In short, we made the cardinal mistake of underestimating the task.

We lost quick wickets at the top of the order and just couldn't come back later so that we were all out for 140 in 52 overs. Greenidge was bowled offering no shot to the inswing bowler, Sandhu. Haynes drove on the up and was caught at mid-off. Gomes and Bacchus edged wide ones and Lloyd, struggling with a muscle he damaged in the semi-final, needed a runner and was caught at mid-on for 8. The decisive wicket was Viv Richards. He was in great form throughout the tournament and looked as if he would win the final on his own with a succession of brilliant shots. He kept on hitting boundary after boundary, seven in all and three in Madan Lal's first over. Suddenly, he top-edged a hook off Madan Lal and Kapil Dev ran back from mid-wicket to take a well-judged catch.

You could hear the roar from the Indian supporters in the crowd all the way to Bombay. The silence of our supporters was equally deafening although, when the end came, a few phrases issued in our direction about our performance were clear and caustic. Defeat was unthinkable to the thousands of West Indians in England who came with their posters prematurely proclaiming: 'The Cup is ours'. They were very upset now that it wasn't.

We had thrown away our world championship and missed out on the hat-trick we were aiming for. There is no shame in being beaten by a better team while you've tried your best but the disappointment of that sunny Saturday afternoon is still vivid in my memory.

There were sharp recriminations afterwards in our

dressing-room as players started apportioning blame. When someone said the batsmen had let us down, one of the batsmen retaliated with the ridiculous comment that the bowlers should have dismissed India more cheaply. There were charges and counter-charges and emotions ran hot. There was also misunderstanding. When Andy Roberts said it was a shame we had lost especially since some had gone out and given their all even though half-fit, he was referring to me as I had a cracked bone in my instep. But the captain took it as a jibe at him for his decision to play in spite of the doubt over his hamstring muscle and he reacted heatedly.

We had a pre-arranged function for friends and supporters at the nearby Westmoreland Hotel after the match and it turned out to be a very sombre occasion, especially when Clive Lloyd publicly announced his resignation as West Indies captain. The defeat was a devastating blow for him most of all. He cherished the goal of leading his team to the Cup for the third time and his decision to quit was obviously brought on by frustration. The next morning, the team broke up as most of us had to get back to our county and league teams and it was left to Allan Rae, then president of the West Indies Board, to sum up the feelings of the players when he persuaded Clive to think over his decision more dispassionately. Thankfully he did, and he was back at the helm when we set out for India later that year to avenge ourselves. But I'm sure none of us will ever get over that World Cup final in 1983.

The 1983–84 tour of India was my first to the country and I approached it a little sceptically. I had heard it was a tough grind, with lots of travelling, pitches that were specially prepared for spinners and the likelihood of being struck down by 'Delhi Belly', the food poisoning that gave India a bad name among touring cricketers. Such stories tend to be embellished and, once I got accustomed to the place, I had an enjoyable tour. In some of the smaller towns, accommodation and food left something to be desired. But that is true of most of the countries I visited. Certainly the hotels in the major cities compared with any I've stayed in anywhere. One surprise was the variation in the weather, very hot in some matches such as the Tests at Kanpur and Bombay, quite cool in others, and decidedly chilly in our first one-day international at Srinagar in Kashmir.

I duly got my touch of 'Delhi Belly' but it didn't last long. On the rest day of the second Test in Delhi, I ordered what I thought would be a harmless glass of lemonade at a restaurant only to become violently ill during the night. Apparently it was mixed with unboiled pipe water. I had to spend the next day at the hotel, having injections, and eat nothing more substantial than yoghurt and fruit for the next few days.

It was an intensive tour with six Tests and five one-day internationals in addition to the up-country games. By the end, we had been to nineteen different cities across that huge country in the two-and-a-half months we spent there. It is the kind of schedule international cricketers have to learn to live with but I came to regard travelling as one of the perks of the game. Few people other than cricketers have the chance to visit such a variety of countries for such long periods as I did during my career. I knew some players had a terrible fear of flying and you had to feel sorry for them as they took off, sweating profusely, fear etched on their faces and desperately clutching the arm-rest. I never had that problem and actually got a thrill from travelling.

For us, and Clive Lloyd especially, the 1983–84 tour of India was a chance to put the World Cup behind us. We had a fierce determination and at no stage were we in danger of defeat. I found that the long-held theory that India was a graveyard for fast bowlers was largely a myth. In fact, Kapil Dev, the Indian captain, complained to the groundsmen in the first Test at Kanpur that the pitch suited us as it was too hard and had too much grass on it. There was also plenty of green in the third Test wicket at Ahmedabad, which was staging its first Test, and we won both comfortably, bowling India out for 207 and 164 at Kanpur, and 241 and 103 at Ahmedabad. Their lowest total of the series came at Eden Gardens in Calcutta when they were routed for 90 in their second innings to lose by an innings and 46 runs. It was a very good batting pitch and a record ninth-wicket stand of 161 between Clive Lloyd, who was unbeaten on 161, and Andy Roberts was the basis of our total of 377. When India batted a second time, mist hung low in the early morning air, as it often does in Calcutta, and the ball wobbled around in the air. They had no answer to Malcolm Marshall's pace and movement and he bowled through the innings to take six for 37. Bombay, Delhi and Madras were all ideal for batting but I never came across the kind of slow, turning, bounceless pitches I had been led to expect.

This was the tour on which I shortened my run and on which Marshall unmistakeably took over as the spearhead of our attack. In the West Indies, earlier in the year, Marshall had been first change as Andy and I had used the new ball but, even then, he was the fastest of us. He was at his peak in India. He bowled with real pace and hostility, even when pitches were flat, and still had the skill to swing it around when conditions warranted at Calcutta. His 33 wickets were one more than Roberts' 32 on the 1974–75 tour, the record for a West Indies bowler in India. I found it interesting to listen to Wes Hall who was our manager. He first toured India back in 1958–59 when he and Roy Gilchrist did all the damage, Wes with 30 wickets in five Tests and

Gillie 26 in four. So where did the myth that India is a spinner's paradise and a fast bowler's hell come from?

I quickly settled into my change of style, off a reduced run, at reduced pace, and took wickets so consistently that I had 30 after five Tests, even though I only once took five wickets in an innings, at Bombay. I drew a blank in the final Test which was spoiled by rain and a couple of incidents involving umpiring decisions.

We had been forewarned that the umpiring might lean towards the home team but I'd played enough by now to know this was generally true everywhere. After the third Test, Clive Lloyd was moved to describe the umpires as two of the worst he had come across, a pretty sweeping indictment. But it was never the controversial issue it was in Australia in 1975–76 or in New Zealand in 1980.

The major 'incident' occurred in the final Test in which Sunil Gavaskar went past Don Bradman's record number of Test centuries with his thirtieth, converting it into an eventual 236 not out. It had been a difficult series for Gavaskar. He was out to the first ball of the match at Calcutta and was bitterly criticised in the press and by the fans when he virtually threw his hand away in the second innings with an atrocious shot. With five failures on the trot, he asked to be put in at no. 4 in the order in the last Test. It was a sure sign of his loss of confidence but he might as well have opened for Marshall took the first two wickets without a run on the board. India were again in danger of falling apart at 92 for five in reply to our 313 when Gavaskar edged Marshall's second ball of the fourth day to third slip. Harper held a low, clean catch but, as Gavaskar stood his ground, the umpire said not out. It was a blatant mistake, if that is what it was, and we made our feelings known by refusing to acknowledge Gavaskar's various landmarks. There was a great deal of criticism in the press of what was termed our unsportsmanlike behaviour but nothing of Gavaskar's sportsmanship in influencing a not-out decision for a clear catch.

I let my emotions get the better of me later in the match over an episode when I was batting. I had added valuable runs for the eighth wicket with Marshall when I got a faint touch to the last ball before the tea break from Kapil Dev. To my surprise, no-one appealed and, as we walked off, I asked Syed Kirmani, their wicketkeeper, what had happened. He thought there was a touch, he said, but since no-one else appealed, he didn't either. When I confirmed I'd touched it, we laughed and he shrugged it off as just one of those things. On resumption, it took only a few balls for the Indians to get their own back. As soon as I was struck on the pad, there was a huge appeal even though I was well outside the off-stump and a long way down. I was convinced Kirmani had filled the umpire in on our tea-time conversation and he was now making sure that I *was* out. I was pretty upset and when I got a chance to bowl at Kirmani late in the match, I let fly with a series of bouncers and even a few beamers. It was an uncalled for reaction and, when I reflected on it, I wasn't proud of myself. I got on well with most of the Indian players, not least Kirmani himself, a likeable character whose shaved head made him so distinctive.

I suppose I never did come to terms with poor umpiring and there is no more irritating feeling in the game than to have the umpire shake his head when you know he should have raised his finger, or vice versa. It is worse when the batsman is someone like Gavaskar who was the most difficult batsman to dislodge once the conditions suited him. You just tried to be economical and, once he got past 30 or 40, you hoped he took a single early in the over so you could get at the other batsman. He was very sound and technically correct and, like the other great opposition opener of my time, Geoff Boycott, had tremendous powers of concentration. Unlike Boycott, however, he seemed keen only when conditions suited him. If the ball was bouncing or moving about a lot, he didn't seem to value his wicket all that dearly.

On any cricket tour, with its packed itinerary, there is virtually no time for sight-seeing and I was disappointed that I didn't get to see the Taj Mahal. Professional cricketers are usually not too interested in such cultural opportunities but those who had been on previous tours said it was something special. We did get to visit the Sikh Golden Temple in Amritsar even at a time when it was the centre of a dangerous confrontation between the government and Sikh extremists. The Temple, in fact, was occupied by the Sikh leader and his followers as we toured, so I could relate to the news, some months later, of the storming of the Temple by troops and the death of many Sikhs who were in it at the time.

Although I had heard of the vast size of Indian crowds and the passionate way they follow their cricket, seeing it at first-hand was a real experience. They packed the grounds everywhere and were even more fickle than West Indian crowds. Kapil Dev, the Indian captain, was pelted with oranges and other debris and the team bus was stoned after the Calcutta Test. The manner of India's defeat and the overall performance in the series was even raised in Parliament and it was to cost Kapil Dev the captaincy – another one to fall to West Indian pressure! Just a few months earlier, Kapil and his players were feted as national heroes after their World Cup triumph in England.

Kapil's influence lifted Indian cricket to new heights in the 1980s. He was a natural athlete, a marvellous bowler of raw ability, capable of putting the ball more or less where he wanted, and he moved it around. He didn't have the pace of some of his contemporaries from other countries but his control and movement made him just as effective. He seldom wasted time with tailenders. Potentially a very good batsman, his hit-and-miss approach didn't do his potential any favours but, when things were going his way, he could devastate any bowling.

I got the impression that he wasn't comfortable in the team at all times, and fed up with the politics that pervade Indian cricket. He often went out and did whatever he felt like doing, regardless of the position of the match. In a more settled team, his record might have been even more impressive.

For all the people's anger at their team's performance, they retained a fanatical attachment to the game. Anytime we ventured out of our hotel, we were sure to be quickly surrounded by cricket fans, identifying players and asking for autographs. On one occasion, Pal Ganguli, an Indian friend who had lived in Jamaica and coached the Jamaica hockey team, took Clive Lloyd and his wife, Waveney, and me and my girlfriend, Yvonne, to select some items from a jeweller he knew in Calcutta. When we tried to leave, there was such a crowd surrounding the car, asking for our autographs, they had to send for the police.

After the shock of the World Cup, the tour revitalised Clive Lloyd and added a very productive year to his career, both as player and captain. While his resignation after the defeat at Lord's in June was undoubtedly made on an emotional impulse, I believe some self-doubt remained when he arrived in India – about his motivation, about his fitness, about his form. They were quickly dispelled by his own success as much as that of the team. He seemed to take on a new lease of life and was seldom out of the runs, often getting them in difficult situations. He hit 103 at Delhi, in addition to his unbeaten 161 at Ahmedabad, and often pulled the team out of a hole. A triumphant final year lay ahead of him.

CHAPTER 17

Partners in pace

West Indies' fast bowling philosophy was already well established but the tour of India in 1983 further emphasised the strength and depth of our reserves.

Joel Garner was unavailable as he was having treatment on his right shoulder which had troubled him for some time, and Colin Croft had committed himself to Lawrence Rowe's rebel team to South Africa. Still, the selectors could include six fast bowlers in the touring party of sixteen. Winston Davis, the lively Vincentian, was first picked in the previous home season and was retained, Wayne Daniel was recalled for the first time in seven years and Eldine Baptiste from Antigua was introduced for the first time. All had experience of county cricket and joined Andy Roberts, Malcolm Marshall and myself.

It was to be Roberts' last Test series. While the plentiful supply of contenders may have prompted the selectors to look elsewhere, the way he was shunted aside was unbecoming treatment for such a great bowler and one who had given such service to the game.

Prior to that tour, Andy had been our senior bowler throughout his career. No matter who else was in the team, he was the one who bowled the first over, without question. He had the respect and admiration of team-mates and opponents alike because he was a great bowler, full stop. He would probably have retained his place in India but for a decision he took himself.

He was not fully fit leading up to the first Test and, even though he passed a fitness test on the morning of the match to the satisfaction of the selectors, he himself wasn't convinced he was up to a five-day match. So he asked to be left out. He was ready again for the second Test but, when he was again omitted, he looked at it philosophically. 'Well, we won the first Test so perhaps they don't want to change a winning team,' he told me. When he was left out of the third Test as well, he began to read the signals and was decidedly troubled by them.

We were at the regular pre-Test meeting in manager Wes Hall's room when the team was announced. Immediately the formalities were over, Andy left and went back to his room. You didn't have to be a psychologist to know he was upset and disappointed. Usually, he would have stayed on to have a chat, perhaps watch a video and have a glass or two of his favourite drink, orange juice, from which he got his nickname, 'Fruity'. When I got back to our room somewhat later, I expected him to be sleeping. Instead, I found all the lights on and Andy in his bed staring at the ceiling. It was the type of situation in which I really didn't know what to say. To be honest, I don't think Andy wanted me to say anything.

Whenever Wes Hall and Clive Lloyd tried to approach him after that, he wouldn't take them on. He was too cut up by what he saw as the unfair way he was treated. His relationships with them became uneasy and, during one team meeting, he said something he probably shouldn't have said which only accentuated the tension. Reacting to complaints that those players not in the Test team were being neglected in the nets, he said he would make sure that Richie Richardson, at least, would get his practice. Richie was on his first tour and the only specialist batsman not in the Test side. Since he was from Antigua, Andy's comment was seen as just plain pique at his omission with a little insularity thrown in for good measure. This was not Andy's way at all but the situation was such that misunderstanding developed easily.

Andy eventually did return for the last two Tests and became the third West Indian, after Gary Sobers and Lance Gibbs, to reach the landmark of 200 Test wickets, but now it was Malcolm Marshall who bowled the first over. Andy never seemed to have his heart in it after that. Ironically his major contribution was with the bat when he and Clive Lloyd pulled us out of a tight spot in the first innings of the Calcutta Test with their partnership of 161. Only a few days earlier, he learned he had been dropped for the later tour of Australia. Although he returned home to have a good Shell Shield season, he never regained his Test place.

I was very close to Andy, so I might have been somewhat biased. But I didn't approve how the whole problem was handled. I regarded Andy as still a fine fast bowler certainly worth his place. If the selectors did not see it that way and felt he was coming to the end of the road, Clive could have had a word with him and given him the option of leaving the scene of his own accord by retiring. That sort of courtesy should be extended to anyone who has given the kind of service Andy had done. The two had been in the team together since 1974 and enjoyed a close, friendly rapport. It was all the more reason why there should have been communication. The matter was badly handled and only created bad blood between two great players and good friends. It also brought an angry reaction from his many supporters back home who railed against Andy's exclusion.

It was not the first time, nor would it be the last, that our great players would bow out of Test cricket in bitterness. Viv Richards, Gordon Greenidge and Jeffrey Dujon were recently very critical of the West Indies Board and the selectors when they were dropped after their long and distinguished careers. Surely the Board must be conscious of treating those who have given long and faithful service to West Indies cricket fairly and respectfully? Selectors know when a player, however great, no longer fits into their plans and when they want to replace him with someone younger. There is nothing wrong with that, but the player should be advised of the situation and given the option of announcing his retirement rather than having to suffer the indignity of being dropped.

Don't get me wrong. I do not believe players should be petted and pampered. But too many times have I seen our top players hurt and degraded as they hear they have been omitted. My friend, Andy Roberts, was one.

His exit marked the end of an era. He was the cornerstone of the pace policy and was the one who initially carried the other fast bowlers in his slipstream. In the early days he did the bulk of the work and never flinched from it. We just supported him before the four-pronged attack was developed with everyone pitching in and performing as a team.

It never seemed to matter who got the wickets, once the opposition was bowled out, and each man did his fair share of the work. Clive Lloyd had it calculated almost down to the last decimal point how to share the load. As an example, in Australia in 1979–80, Joel Garner had 127.4 overs with 14 wickets, Colin Croft 121.3 overs with 16 wickets, Andy Roberts 112 overs and 11 wickets and I had 111 overs and 14 wickets. To support the point further, I've calculated that Roberts bowled an average of 39 overs per Test over his career, Garner and Croft 38 each, and I got off lightly with 35! Not even the most skilful union negotiator could ask for a more equitable distribution.

We would discuss each other's cricketing problems as they arose for each of us was aware of what the others were capable of. I've pointed out how Andy's advice helped me get my first Test wicket and alter my run. It was the kind of cooperation we had among us all.

Because the sight of four tall, well-built fast bowlers made for a good press photo, a lot was made of us as a quartet. We were all different, in our bowling as well as in our personalities, but there was a close affinity between us that I'm sure contributed greatly to our success.

Garner, known to everyone as 'Big Bird' or just 'Bird', and I also talked a lot about each other's bowling without ever taking it as criticism. There were times when 'Bird' would find it difficult to get the ball to move both ways. He could make it go away through an entire day without cutting one back and vice-versa and, when that happened, I'd suggest swapping around the shiny side of the ball or changing the grip on the seam. Not that it always worked, but that kind of cooperation maintained a strong bond between us. Croft, with his unorthodox action, was one in a thousand and just did his own thing. We knew it was pointless trying to work out just what he was doing, so we let him get on with it, but he was quick to come forward with his observations about batsmen and they were usually spot-on.

I rate Andy Roberts the best of all the fast bowlers I played with or against. You name it, Andy had it. He was strong and serious about his work. Genuinely fast, he developed clever change of pace that was one of his greatest assets. He swung the ball away but could also cut it back sharply. And I never knew a batsman who could competently handle his variety of bouncers, one decidedly faster than the other. Above all, he had a shrewd understanding of what he was about, his brain always ticking as he searched for a batsman's weakness. When he found it, he had the control to exploit it.

Joel Garner was a physical phenomenon. Someone of his size needs to be immensely strong to maintain the demands of fast bowling and he is the only one who has managed it at Test level. His height of 6 feet 7 inches was his main asset and he used it well, varying the steep bounce he could get with his accurate yorker. His Test record is as imposing as his physique, with 259 wickets at an average of 20.97. Yet I feel he sold himself short and could have ended up with closer to 300 wickets. He enjoyed life and contended he needed to relax away from the game. There is nothing wrong with that and 'Bird' was adamant that, even after a night out, he could bowl 35 overs the next day without bother. So he could but, if he had been in tip-top condition, he could have pulled the choke more often and produced more wicket-taking balls instead of being content to bowl accurately all day. A look at his statistics is revealing for he only took five or more wickets in an innings seven times and never ten in a match. He may have seen his role in the quartet more as a stock, rather than shock, bowler. Perhaps it would have been different if he had been the leader of the pack. He was certainly a rare and magnificent bowler, good enough to have taken even more wickets.

Croft was a moody individual. He was difficult to reason with but, once on the field, you could count on him to give 110 per cent all the time. He was immensely strong and was always trying, while his awkward action and delivery made him quite a handful to deal with. He straddled the crease so wide that his left foot would be outside the box on delivery and, from that angle, he would pitch off-stump and still hit off-stump, an impossible ball to play.

It was natural that the relationship should change once the personnel changed. Pop groups seldom rediscover their original magic once they have to replace the drummer or the lead guitarist. The same holds true for sporting teams. It was never quite as open once Andy Roberts and Colin Croft left the scene and things became a little bit more competitive. With so many challengers for places, this was not a bad thing and the chain of fast bowling has been maintained ever since.

I would put our quartet as at its peak between 1979–80, when we toured Australia in the first season following the end of World Series Cricket, and 1981 when England toured the Caribbean. We were all still comparatively young (Andy was the oldest at twenty-nine) yet we all had a lot of experience and were physically at our fittest. We each had a distinctive style so that Clive always had a bowler up his sleeve to suit any eventuality. If one man couldn't do the job, another one could because he was a different type and the constant rotation of the four meant the batsman had to keep adjusting to differences of pace, height, bounce and angle. As he himself has observed, no captain would have wanted more.

In spite of our success or, more correctly, because of it, we were increasingly criticised and the criticism got more strident over the years. The English press especially mounted a virulent campaign to discredit the West Indies and to have the laws changed so as to restrict our main strength, fast bowling.

It claimed that our fast bowling was detrimental

to the game because it slows the over-rate. It said the absence of spin robbed the game of a lot of its charm. All sorts of suggestions were put forward including such ridiculous nonsense as lengthening the pitch and drawing a line of demarcation down the middle. Eventually, the propaganda worked and the ICC was influenced into introducing laws stipulating the minimum number of overs a day in Test cricket at 90, and restricting bouncers to one an over per batsman.

There has always been a law on the books to deal with overuse of bouncers, Law 42, Paragraph 8, and the umpires are there to enforce it. The problem, however, lies not so much with the umpires or the old law but with the lack of technique of modern batsmen to contend with good, aggressive fast bowling. It is true that several batsmen have been hit by our fast bowlers over the years but such injuries are not confined to Test matches against the West Indies alone. There have been plenty in ordinary county matches as well. More often than not, the batsman who is hit takes his eyes off the ball or plays too low. Very few West Indians have been struck, even when playing against their own fast bowlers in the Red Stripe Cup, and I can't recall the best players such as Javed Miandad, Sunil Gavaskar, Barry Richards or David Gower having fingers or arms broken. When a top player is hit, more often than not a pitch with uneven bounce is in there somewhere, such as the one in Trinidad when Graham Gooch had his finger broken in 1990 and that at Sabina Park in recent years where so many have suffered. I found it interesting that almost all the current and recent Test players from every country decried the ICC's new bouncer rule. Imran Khan called it 'one of the most brainless pieces of legislation ever passed' by the ICC and Gary Sobers said simply: 'I really can't believe such a law could ever be passed by anyone who knows anything about cricket'.

Instead of trying to manipulate the laws to try to bring West Indies cricket down to their level, the detractors should be sorting out the game in their countries. It should not be for teams strong in fast bowling to be handicapped by a change in laws that have served the game for over a hundred years but for the others to lift their standards. Far from saving the game by bringing back spin, such measures only serve to encourage mediocrity and devalue its standard. If spinners are good enough, they will demand their places on merit, not by artificial manipulation.

Fast bowling is an indelible part of the West Indian cricketing culture. It is a tradition that stretches back to our earliest beginnings. The exploits of the greats of the 1920s and 1930s, like George John, George Francis, Herman Griffith, Learie Constantine and Leslie Hylton, were passed on to future generations just as those of Wes Hall, Charlie Griffith and Roy Gilchrist were passed on to those of my vintage. It is a continuing sequence and it is more than sheer coincidence that so many were ready to fill the places vacated when Andy Roberts, Joel Garner and I went into retirement.

Young men grow up wanting to bowl fast. Even those who don't but who have the attributes of height and strength are quickly converted, as the stories of Curtly Ambrose, Ian Bishop and Tony Gray indicate. Ambrose's main game was basketball before friends in his village in Antigua could persuade him not to let the advantage of his height go to waste and to take up fast bowling. In their native Trinidad, not known for producing fast bowlers, Bishop was an opening batsman at school and Gray was a soccer goalkeeper.

Our total dependence on fast bowling and our remarkable record of success through the 1980s could be traced back to 1976 so that those born since the 1960s have grown up knowing nothing else. If they are aware of them at all, our great spinners, Sonny Ramadhin, Alf Valentine and Lance Gibbs, are no more than names from the misty pages of history to the modern generation. The fast bowlers of their age are here and now, on Test match grounds or on TV screens, hailed as heroes and role models.

West Indians are proud of that heritage and we take umbrage when it is queried on specious grounds. It also grinds when the impression is given that our success is not based on skill, planning and effort but simply on intimidation and brute force. The negative comments have come mainly in the British media and contain undisguised elements of envy and resentment. I need only quote from an article in *Wisden Cricket Monthly* prior to the West Indies' tour of England in 1991, written by the editor, David Frith, and splashed on the sports page of the *Daily Mirror*, to make the point:

'Another invasion is upon us by a West Indies team which is the most fearsome, the most successful and the most unpopular in the world. Their game is founded on vengeance and violence and fringed on arrogance. The only mercy is that they're not bringing their umpires.'

It is easy to say we should just ignore such comments but I wonder if any team in any sport has been subjected to such an orchestrated campaign of defamation as the West Indies had to endure for so long. Could it have had something to do with the standards of excellence we set ourselves and the results we managed to achieve?

Fast bowling, of course, was an integral part of our success but so, too, was the brilliant and vital support we received from our wicketkeepers and slip fielders. When we ran up to bowl, we only needed to hear that snick because we knew it almost certainly guaranteed a wicket! It did not cross our minds that it might be dropped. This is not to say that one didn't get away now and again but it was always a surprise when it did. There were times at other levels when I would hope the slip catch would stick. In the West Indies team, I always expected it to. Since nine times out of ten it did, I could accept the odd missed chance without the frustration that overcomes any bowler when catch after catch is put down.

Such perfection was not a fluke or ordained from above. It came from purposeful hours of practice that honed reflexes and increased confidence. Even on the morning before a day's play in a Test, we would have a session on the field and in the nets that invariably drew a big crowd to marvel at the catches that were taken. There was always the danger of getting a bad knock or two on the hands and fingers but, once you were catching properly, that was no bother. Practice makes perfect and our attitude was that it was no sense lobbing the ball to the fielders who would then go into the middle to find it flying off the edge at pace.

The exercise not only perfected our slip catching but produced extraordinary all-round fielders. Lloyd was rated one of the best cover-points the game has known before his serious back injury during the Rest of the World tour in 1972 confined him to the slips where he was equally brilliant. He repeatedly said that practice could turn almost any cricketer into a good fielder. Some were blessed with better eyesight or more athleticism or simply bigger hands than others and were outstanding anywhere. But we could always boast that we didn't have a weak fielder in the team. If there was one, he would have stuck out like a sore thumb.

In my time, there were no better fielders than Viv

Richards and Roger Harper. They were as safe and as spectacular in the slips as in the outfield. Both were such great athletes. They were fast runners, had strong throws and exceptional hand-eye coordination. Lance Gibbs, Roy Fredericks and Joel Garner were specialists in the gully where Garner's huge hands and long reach made it almost impossible to pass him. Lawrence Rowe and Alvin Kallicharran were alongside Lloyd when I first came into the team and, later, Richards, Gordon Greenidge and Richie Richardson made that area secure. Short-leg is a crucial position for the fast bowlers and the alertness of the specialists we had there gave our attack a new dimension as so many batsmen seem unable to play properly the lifting ball between hip and shoulder height. Desmond Haynes, Faoud Bacchus and little Gus Logie snared dozens of wickets for us with their sharp reflexes and their sheer courage in that position.

Nor is catching alone important. A bowler's specific plan to a specific batsman can be completely disrupted if he gets a single he shouldn't have had and is allowed to move off the strike. That didn't happen very often with the West Indies in the 1980s.

I found it disturbing to note a decline in these standards during recent series against England and Australia and then, even more markedly, in the World Cup in Australia and New Zealand. Covering the series for the media, it seemed to me that not as much attention was being paid to fielding and catching practice as before and a lot of vital edged chances were put down.

No matter how strong the attack, it needs the support of its fielders. It may be a cliché but catches do win matches, and this is one aspect of West Indies cricket that we will have to continue paying attention to, as much as our Board will have to guard against attempts to emasculate all fast bowlers – metaphorically speaking, of course.

CHAPTER 18

A fast bowler's philosophy

I became a fast bowler more by circumstance than choice. I knew it was time to change and bowl quick like everyone else when the boys in our knockabout games at Redhills Oval stuck their unprotected legs in front of the stumps with impunity against my tossed up off-spin knowing they could neither be lbw, because there were no umpires, nor hurt. Even if subconsciously, I realised then that one of the key elements in fast bowling is intimidation. When someone is running in to hurl a ball at you from a distance of twenty-two yards, he doesn't necessarily have to bounce it at your throat to be menacing.

I didn't take very long, either, to appreciate that pace alone wasn't sufficient for success. In matches I played for Melbourne Club and when I got to Kingston College, batsmen wore pads, gloves and boxes, if not yet helmets, and the pitches were flat and properly prepared, not like the raw ground at Redhills Oval.

It meant that I had to learn to bowl and I was lucky in the guidance and advice I got. Ironically, a lot came from two spin bowlers at Melbourne, Bruce Wellington, an orthodox left-armer who played for Jamaica, and Arthur Barrett, a leg-spinner good enough to play six Tests in the early 1970s. It was Bruce who determined my grip on the ball and Arthur who introduced me to the inswinger – through the influence of my mother.

In the coaching books which Dad provided, the approved grip showed fingers over the seam, slightly slanted and pointing towards second slip for the out-swinger and towards fine-leg for the inswinger. That was all well and good but I found I could only get it to outswing that way.

In one particular match at Kirkvine, on a pitch with a little grass, I was tilting the seam as per instructions and the ball was swinging away miles, out of control. I was then fourteen and couldn't understand what I was doing wrong. After all, I was following the book. When Bruce Wellington stepped in to help, I showed him how I was holding the ball and, right away, he told me to forget it.

'Just hold it with the seam straight between the fingers. It'll still swing but you'll have better control,' he said. 'It's not the grip that makes it swing as much as your body movement.' So it proved. But even though I could now keep it on target, I still only bowled out-swingers. What was more frustrating was that almost every time the ball found the edge, the slip fielders would drop the catch. This is where Mum came in.

'If they're going to keep dropping like that you better had try some inswingers to hit the stumps,' she suggested. It seemed logical enough and Arthur Barrett taught me how to do it by delivering from wide of the crease, opening up my chest a little and pushing the ball in on the angle. I still held it with the seam straight up but found I could now bowl both the outswinger and the inswinger, even if some of the time it was an optical illusion and had a lot to do with angles.

After that, I very seldom altered the way I held the ball, only slanting the seam a little when there was nothing in the pitch and nothing much happening. After I got into the West Indies team, Andy Roberts suggested I place the seam crossways for the bouncer, as he and

Comrades-in-arms – Andy Roberts and I relax in the dressing-room.

(*Above*) One for the book. Holding flourishes the bat in the Headingley Test of 1981. (*Patrick Eagar*)

(*Below*) Garner and Croft hold Lloyd aloft after his match-winning 77 not out at Adelaide, third Test, 1981–82 (*Sydney Herald*)

(*Above*) Viv Richards – a
batting genius with three
different strokes for every
ball (*David Munden*)
(*Below*) Ahmedabad, 1983:
I am Man of the Match.
Who said India was a fast
bowlers' graveyard?

(*Above*) Nice and relaxed, eyes on the target, I am ready to deliver against Western Australia at Perth on the 1984–85 tour
(*West Australian*)
(*Below*) My captain and me: setting the field during the 1985 World Championship of Cricket
(*Adrian Murrell, All Sports*)

(*Above*) Changing times: characterised by England's David Smith, helmeted and standing with bat held high (*Gordon Brooks*)

(*Below*) 'Happiness is . . . an England wicket,' in this case Allan Lamb's at Port-of-Spain, fourth Test, 1986 (*Willie Alleyne*)

(*Above*) Javed Miandad,
Pakistan's leading batsman
for twenty years, on the
attack (*Gordon Brooks*)
(*Below*) three fast bowlers
from Jamaica: Patrick
Patterson, Courtney Walsh
and Michael Holding

(*Above*) Treating one of the horses to sugar; (*below*) Holdings' Pavilion at Melbourne Club – the apostrophe appropriately covers my father, my mother and me (*Dellmar H.G. Samuels*)

(*Above*) The new boss in attendance at Michael Holding's Service Station in New Kingston. As my mother always said: 'There's life after cricket' (*Dellmar H.G. Samuels*); even, you might say (*below*) commentating on Channel Nine with Ian Chappell (*PBL Marketing*)

most fast bowlers did, but I then found I had no control over which side the ball would pitch on. I hated it to land on the shiny side so I quickly abandoned the idea and got back to using body action, arm swing, and the width of the crease for variation.

While the new ball has the advantage of being harder and bouncier, the established theory is that the old ball will swerve more if one side is kept polished and smooth while the other is scuffed up by normal wear and tear. While I had to put plenty of body movement into my delivery to make the new ball move around, I found I could dictate the swing more readily when it was older simply by gripping the rougher side in the direction I wanted. The explanation is that the movement is caused by friction through the air. Another, more recent contention is that it goes the opposite way, so-called 'reverse swing', but this can only be possible because perspiration has been applied to one side which is, therefore, heavier. Colin Croft was a great one for applying perspiration to keep one side smooth but I hated to feel a wet ball. So did Andy Roberts and Joel Garner, and we had to keep telling him off.

The current Pakistani fast bowlers, Waqar Younis and Wasim Akram, have reaped tremendous success recently by making the old ball move prodigiously with 'reverse swing', which has led to allegations, first made by New Zealand and the West Indies during their Test series in Pakistan late in 1990, and even more controversially in England in 1992, that they and the Pakistan team are deliberately and illegally tampering with the ball.

I have no way of knowing whether Waqar and Wasim, or anyone else these days, doctors the ball or not or how they do it, but I do know it was common practice for as long as I played. Bowlers used their thumbnails to lift the seam to make it more prominent and I've seen, in county cricket in England, a few apply lip salve to their trousers to help keep one side of the ball shiny all day, an illegal tactic that seemed unnecessary since the ball moves around naturally in England as it is.

For those who knew what was going on, it was quite evident on TV that bowlers were using their fingernails and playing with the seam as they went back to their mark. They would contend they were just cleaning the seam of any mud or dirt but it still amounted to interference with the ball. And this was not confined to bowlers of any one country. It was universal and I wouldn't pretend that I was entirely innocent.

Yet it was never an issue because it was an accepted part of the game and no-one ever really overdid it. I never saw an umpire warn a bowler for ball abuse and there were never any complaints. The furore has erupted lately because, it is said, the offenders have gone beyond meddling with the seam and are taking bottle stoppers, nails and even pocket knives on to the field to scratch it up. If this is so, and known to be so, then I agree that firm action should be taken by the authorities, and quickly.

Throughout my career, my run-up was, so to speak, my trademark. I was never strong and powerful and, to generate maximum pace, needed to build up rhythm. It meant an extraordinarily long approach but I felt very comfortable with it and rate it the most crucial factor in my bowling. Big, strapping men such as Andy Roberts and Sylvester Clarke could gain their speed from sheer strength but others with more streamlined physiques, such as Dennis Lillee, Malcolm Marshall and myself, depended on our timing and coordination. My approach increased year by year until I finally settled it in my last two years at Kingston College. I would measure out twenty-five paces, put down my marker and then go back another ten paces in which I would get into full stride. It remained that way until I shortened it in India in 1983.

My weight distribution, between 179 and 185 pounds spread over a frame of 6 feet 3½ inches, meant that I was comparatively light on my feet and my track and field training helped develop a sprinter's stride. It was a combination that instigated Dickie Bird's nickname 'Whispering Death', and Geoff Boycott's 'Rolls-Royce' analogy. But not everyone appreciated the length of the run and there is a picture in the 1981 edition of *Wisden*, the caption of which illustrates the point: 'The reason why the West Indies over-rate was the slowest ever. M. A. Holding, in the Headingley Test match, approaches the end of his long walk back to his mark. The attitudes of the fielders are indicative of the tedium.'

Almost all modern fast bowlers have been plagued by the problem of overstepping the front crease on delivery stride and, with our fleet of fast bowlers, the West Indies have suffered more than any other team. But I have no sympathy with those who repeatedly transgress. They just don't work hard enough on their run-ups and that's unprofessional. It certainly is no reason to revert to the old law which judged a no-ball by the placement of the back foot, not the front, as is now being suggested. The length of the pitch should be the same for everyone and no-one should be able to gain an advantage because his longer stride allows him to deliver the ball from twenty yards. I certainly have no problem with the law as it stands although so many fast bowlers seem to.

Once you're bowling no-balls, it must enter your mind at some stage of your run-up that this one is going to be another. Once that happens, it means you're not concentrating fully on putting the ball where you want it and I've seen experienced bowlers completely undermined by the problem. As a teenager, I got into the habit of straddling the crease on delivery and, being small at the time, it meant I landed well behind the front line. I felt at ease that way and, far from being a handicap, I regarded delivering with a few inches to spare as an asset. Since I didn't have to concern myself about being called, I could maintain my rhythm and rest assured that, even if I went forward a couple of inches seeking extra pace, I was still all right.

On my first tour of Australia, the senior players noticed I was putting my front foot down with as much as a foot to spare and they worked to get me up closer. I didn't bowl a no-ball all tour and when I was called for the first time in my career the following summer in the West Indies' match against the MCC at Lord's, Clive Lloyd was so flabbergasted, he rushed up to find out what was going on. He suspected the umpire was getting on my case early in the tour until I explained that I didn't have proper spikes in my boots, that I was showing off a bit on my first appearance at Lord's and that my front foot had, indeed, slid over the line. Gradually, I did get closer and overstepped on occasions but it was never a concern. Bowlers have enough to cope with as it is without having to worry about something else.

Like everything in cricket, concentration is essential in bowling. Even before I got on to the field, I determined my general strategy. Whether the batsman was right- or left-handed, I would think first of the off stump, aiming for a reasonably negative length, not up for the drive or short for the cut. The purpose was to put the ball where I wanted, keep the batsman on the defensive and gain some confidence. That established,

I would then increase pace and experiment, but the first task was to establish a rhythm. There were times, of course, when I deviated from the established plan, such as in the opening over to Geoff Boycott in the Barbados Test of 1981, but I never tried to bowl flat out unless I felt right within myself.

After I got to my mark, I tried to be fully relaxed. Once I'd established that, all I thought about was where I wanted the ball to go and what I wanted it to do. I already knew who the batsman was and what field I had set, so my focus could then be solely on delivering the ball. It was in between deliveries and in between overs that I'd think about tactics, playing through in my mind exactly what had happened with the previous ball or the previous over, how the batsman had handled it and deciding what to serve up next.

With experience, and often help from team-mates, I could quickly assess batsmen's strengths and weaknesses and know what to expect from them.

It was a waste of energy, for instance, bowling Geoff Boycott a short ball to get him to cut or hook. He eliminated the slightest risk and would just get out of the way and let it pass. If you got him out, it would have to be when he was defending against a good one, not attacking a bad one. On the other hand, I could be sure that Ian Chappell would take on any challenge. The difference was that you could get away with a bad ball to batsmen like Boycott who were keener on wearing you down than demoralising you. Others, like Ian Chappell, Viv Richards and Clive Lloyd, set out to attack and destroy the bowler. I always felt more relaxed bowling to the Boycotts of this world. With someone like Ian Chappell, the adrenaline pumped faster. I knew I had a chance but I also knew I could be in for a good caning. Every ball I expected something to happen, a challenge that was always exciting.

Like Richards, Ian had the ability to smash similar balls in different directions with different strokes and utterly to humiliate any bowler when he was 'on song'. The WSC tour of the West Indies in 1979 typified his approach to batting. In the Barbados Supertest, he was in brilliant touch, cutting and hooking for 61 in the first innings and 86 in the second, a lot of his boundaries off my bowling. In the next Supertest in Port-of-Spain, he went for the hook early in both innings against me, mistimed the shot and lobbed return catches both times, out for 1 and 0. He wasn't the genius Richards was but he remained the best non-West Indian batsman I've bowled to. His brother, Greg, was far more orthodox and predictable and enjoyed a better record but, like other Australian players of that generation, he benefited from Ian's unselfish approach.

Strangely, the batsman I most hated bowling to would not rate very highly in world cricket but, whether he was in for county, Northamptonshire, or for country, England, I always found it difficult to deal with Peter Willey because he was so utterly unorthodox. No-one in the game stood as square-on as he did, both feet facing the bowler, and somehow I couldn't work out the correct way to bowl to him. It's not to say I didn't get him out a few times but he was always a fierce competitor, difficult to dislodge, and I hated to see him coming in.

My career coincided with the explosion of one-day cricket and I discuss its effects on the game in a later chapter. Many players used to complain that it was too physically demanding and perhaps too many matches are now played. Personally, I found it presented an entirely different challenge to the traditional game and I relished it. It was devised purely as action-packed entertainment for the spectators and that means plenty of runs rather than plenty of wickets, which, in turn, means limitations on field-placing, the quota of overs and the length and width of the bowling. So the bowler has to accept that the rules are stacked against him.

It certainly doesn't call for a great degree of skill, except being able to bowl as straight as possible, but it does improve a bowler's thinking power and control. I soon learned that it was futile going into a one-day match with any preconceived strategy except to aim for middle stump on a full length. Even that had to sometimes change halfway through the run-up as the batsman backed away towards the leg-side or advanced down the wicket – 'giving the charge', as it is termed. It meant I had to be constantly thinking, and flexible.

It is a completely different game to Test or first-class cricket and I thoroughly enjoyed it because of that difference. There were times when I felt more satisfaction coming off with 20 runs from my ten overs in a one-day international than if I'd taken three or four wickets in a Test.

The fact is I enjoyed bowling, through and through.

CHAPTER 19

Believing in ourselves

There is no other competition like Australia's World Series Cup with its coloured uniforms, white balls, floodlights, boisterous crowds. This was now our objective when we left India on New Year's Day, 1984.

As usual three teams were involved (Pakistan was the other) and we each played ten first-round matches leading to the best-of-three finals. The concept was a carry-over from Packer days and became enormously popular. But it placed great physical and mental demands on the players and the majority didn't really enjoy it, partly because of the almost daily air travel. Collis King once described it as 'a 33-record played at 45-speed' and, with so much action packed into limited time, it called for instant energy. I always found it a challenge but there was no way it could provide the true test of cricketing ability like the longer, traditional format. The bottom line is that the turnstiles tick over and the money rolls in. During that six weeks stint in Australia, we pulled in crowds of 86,133, a one-day record at the time, and 72,000 in two matches against Australia at the Melbourne Cricket Ground, and there were several sell-outs elsewhere. It became the usual pattern for one-day cricket. As they say, 'bums on seats' pay the wages, so who are the players to complain?

But we did complain, vehemently, at the end of

that series on an issue that had nothing to do with the playing schedule and everything to do with dollar bills. It arose out of what we, and almost everyone else, perceived as a convenient interpretation of the rules following a tie in the second match of the finals. We won the first final match easily by nine wickets but the second ended with scores level at 222 when Australia's last man, Craig McDermott, was run out off the last ball by Jeffrey Dujon as he tried to steal a bye. Unlike one-day competitions in England and the West Indies, there was no provision here for deciding the winner on the number of wickets lost. We would have won the match on that count but it was officially a tie. The conditions did state that the team with the most victories in the first round would be the winners if the final series was 'incomplete' and, on that basis, we reckoned we should have been presented with the Cup and the $50,000 prize money there and then.

But no. The Australian Board ruled that a third match should be played, even though we would win the Cup, whatever happened. It was ludicrous and we were adamant we would not be party to it. Several prominent Australians, among them Ian Chappell, felt the same way. Meetings went on late into the night to try to resolve the matter and, in the end, manager Wes Hall came back to tell us he had agreed we would play. Clive Lloyd was not included in the discussions and was furious that Wes should have accepted what he saw as an unprincipled move by the Australians. They compounded the foolishness by putting up an 'incentive' of $30,000 for the third match. Following on from India, it was the end of a long, hard tour. Only a few hours earlier, we were convinced it was over and we had won the Cup. Now to hear that we would have to go back out the next day in what were dubious circumstances made it very difficult to find motivation.

It was almost impossible to raise a side at all since several players opted out with niggling injuries. Neither Clive nor Viv Richards could turn out so it gave me the chance to captain the West Indies for the first time in my career. The fans seemed to see through the whole business and less than 20,000 came out for the third match, compared with over 40,000 for the tied match. We won it easily, by six wickets, Gus Logie and Jeffrey Dujon both batting superbly to get into the 80s. But it was a mystery how we did it. Everybody was just going through the motions, there was none of the usual 'high-fiving' and hardly any appealing. We just took it as it came. All the same, it gave me a 100 per cent record as West Indies captain!

Within three weeks of our return home, we were facing the Aussies again. Not since 1973, when Ian Chappell's team won 2–0, had they come with a full-strength team. Bobby Simpson's team in 1978 had excluded all the Packer players and, while the Packer tour of 1979 was probably between the two strongest teams at the time, it was not fully representative. In the interim, we had twice been to Australia for shared Test tours and retained the Worrell Trophy in series of three Tests each. So this was the first full meeting between the teams, over five Tests, since 1973.

Those who looked forward to a keen contest were disappointed. The Australians hardly put up a fight. They saved the first two Tests mainly through the dogged batting of Allan Border and the help he got from the tailenders and from the rain, and they were badly beaten in the last three. Throughout the series we did not lose a second-innings wicket.

The one-sided outcome emphasised not only our own strength and self-confidence but also the crushing effect on the Australians of the simultaneous retirements of Greg Chappell, Dennis Lillee and Rodney

Marsh in the preceding series against Pakistan. They were all three greats of their time and they all bowed out together. It left a huge void in each department of the team and threw heavy responsibility on the shoulders of their captain, Kim Hughes. It was to have its repercussions when we toured Australia later in the year.

Australia was a team divided against itself and there was obvious indiscipline, on and off the field, which reflected in their cricket. It took me back to our tour of Australia in 1975–76 and Hughes and the management seemed unable to check the situation. Only Border rose above it, repeatedly keeping us at bay with sheer courage and determination, a role he would fill for Australia for some time to come. He is not a pretty player, a left-hander lacking the style of a Gary Sobers or a David Gower, but once he gets stuck in and reaches 30 or 40, it is the devil to get him out! He has immense powers of concentration and determination and, while he does not have a wide range of shots, he sticks to those he plays best and with least risk. As a former softball player, he is very strong on the cut and pull but, when I was watching him in the West Indies in 1991, I felt he kept them in storage too much, limiting himself to straight-batted shots. We picked up his main weakness in Australia in 1984–85 when we had him caught close in on the leg-side fending lifting balls off his body. But when you saw him standing at the opposite end you knew you had your work cut out.

Another injury, this time a pulled calf muscle, kept me out of the first two Tests and Malcolm Marshall also had to miss the first Test through a muscle strain. Since the selectors had obviously made up their minds that they were through with Andy Roberts, it meant our bowling was below strength and this helped Australia to hold on for their draws in Georgetown and Port-of-Spain. Well into the fourth day, it seemed the third Test in Barbados was also heading for a draw before one of the quickest turn-arounds in my experience brought us victory.

It was initiated by Clive Lloyd. He came in early on the fourth day, took the match by the scruff of the neck and shook it back to life with a run-a-ball 76. In next to no time, we were in the lead by 80 runs and Australia, completely taken aback, utterly collapsed to 97 all out in their second innings. Marshall and I got the ball to move around and keep a little low on a worn pitch. They batted without any purpose and we were home by ten wickets before lunch.

It was a startling turn of events, comparable to the swing in the Kingston Test against India the year before. On that occasion, India were 168 for six at tea on the last day, 165 in the lead. It was an equation that defied a result. Then Andy Roberts took four wickets in two overs and we won by knocking off 172 in 25.2 overs. Both victories were testimony to the belief we held in ourselves in that period, the realisation that we were always capable of making something out of nothing.

Success breeds success and it was that self-confidence that extended our sequence of Test wins over the next two series, in England and in Australia, to a record eleven.

Coming directly from the triumph over Australia in the Caribbean, we found an unsettled England team in a summer of settled weather in 1984. While we had been taking care of Kim Hughes' side, England were going through a tortured time on tours of New Zealand and Pakistan. They came back to sensational allegations in the tabloid press of drug-taking by certain leading players and there were undercurrents of the same kind of dissension in the ranks of the Australians in the West Indies. To compound matters, there was panic-stricken selection that undermined confidence even further. It was a recipe for failure and the outcome was scarcely surprising. It was the first 5–0 drubbing ever inflicted on England at home.

England's selectors made the mistake of looking for instant success. They introduced one player almost as soon as he got a century or a few wickets at county level and, just as quickly, discarded him when he failed in the Test. It is true that those who went to South Africa with the rebel team a few years before were still sitting out their ban, including Graham Gooch, John Emburey and one or two others who would probably have been chosen. That seemed to me all the more reason to try to build a new team, but, instead of sticking with those they thought had the talent and giving them time to develop, they chopped and changed in a vain search for instant returns.

For some inexplicable reason, most teams seem to go through similar periods of selection instability. The West Indies endured it during the bleak days of the 1970s when we played twenty Tests without a win, and England's spell would drag on for some time. Had they stuck to a specific formula, they might well have developed a successful team. It is only now, with somewhat more consistency, that they are coming out of the trough.

Stability was certainly one of the main reasons for the West Indies' extended run. We used only thirteen players throughout the five Tests in that series and would probably have kept the same eleven throughout but for a muscle strain that kept me out of the second Test and Malcolm Marshall's broken thumb that sidelined him for the fourth. In contrast, England picked twenty-one players, some of whom – such as Jonathan Agnew, Andy Lloyd and Paul Terry – were hardly ever seen again. Such confusion was par for the course until recently and extended even to their captains. It was no wonder that their Test team went through terrible times. We defeated them 5–0 again in the Caribbean in 1985–86, another so-called 'blackwash', and 4–0 in England in 1988. In the last half of the 1980s, they lost to every country except Sri Lanka. Clearly, there were other factors but, to my mind, none had a greater effect than muddled selection.

I don't think the result would have been changed in 1984 had England's selection been different, but it would have been somewhat more competitive. As it was, we won the five Tests by an innings and 180 runs, nine wickets, eight wickets, an innings and 64 runs, and 172 runs.

It was an outstanding team performance. Everyone made a contribution of some kind. The attack revolved around the four fast bowlers and Joel Garner, refreshed and rejuvenated after his lay-off from the tour of India in 1983, followed his 31 wickets against Australia in the Caribbean with 29 in England. Malcolm Marshall had 24 and I collected 15 in my four Tests. When we discovered a dry, turning pitch at Old Trafford, we had a surprise up our sleeves as Roger Harper's off-spin bowling was a match-winner with six wickets in the second innings. Harper came into the Test team the year before and was an outstanding young all-rounder who held out great hope for the future. Tall and with a high, if rather stiff, action, his forte was his bowling but he was also a magnificent fielder, one of the best I have seen, a very useful batsman and an intelligent cricketer. It was a loss to the West Indies when his action inexplicably went to pieces and his bowling markedly deteriorated.

There were several memorable individual perform-ances in the series and I stood and watched one of them in awe at the non-striker's end in a one-day international at Old Trafford. I entered the proceedings as the last man with the scoreboard 166 for nine with 15 overs to go. As I passed my partner, Viv Richards, he simply said: 'Don't worry. Just hold on.' For the few deliveries that he allowed me to face, I managed to follow his instructions. In the meantime, he fashioned an astonishing innings, even by his standards. By now, I thought there was nothing Viv could do that would surprise me. I had been there for most of his big innings for the West Indies and knew that when his adrenaline was pumping, he was capable of anything. This innings was unbelievable. He reached 189 not out, still the highest one-day international score on record, faced only 170 balls, and a couple of his five sixes were the biggest I have ever seen. For one, he simply put his left foot forward and swung his hefty bat through the line of a ball from Derek Pringle, the medium-pacer. It just kept going and going, clearing the stand at long-on and landing well beyond. It must have carried a good 120 yards. The second also cleared the stands and almost dropped on to the tracks of the nearby Warwick Road train station. He also hit 24 fours and, in our last wicket stand of 106, there wasn't much need for running. While he scored 93, I contributed 12. I cannot conceive any batsman of any era playing an innings of quite the same ferocious power and self-confidence as Richards did that day. England's bowlers, Bob Willis, Ian Botham, Neil Foster, Geoff Miller and Pringle, were powerless to stop him.

Gordon Greenidge, always most at home in England, scored double-centuries in the Tests at Lord's and Old Trafford and Larry Gomes, after a poor series against Australia in which he had been dropped, came back to average 80 in the Tests with his neat, unfussy, left-handed style. Together, they earned us a victory on the last day at Lord's that delivered a severe psychological blow to England.

England's stock was none too high after the first Test when they were routed for 191 and 235 and we amassed 606, but they fought back strongly in the second at Lord's. The first four days were close and intense and the press was so confident it berated England's batsmen for coming off the field for light on the fourth afternoon when 328 runs ahead with three wickets in hand. Instead, they played safe, continued for 20 minutes on the last day and set us 342 to win. To almost everyone, and certainly the England team, it was unthinkable that we would even contemplate trying for a win. We were one up in the series and most teams would have settled for a draw. The attitude at the team meeting the night before, and in the dressing-room that day, was more positive. We were so sure of ourselves by then that to set out for a draw from the start was not an option. Clive Lloyd told his batsmen to play normally and take things one step at a time. Another injury kept me out of that match but I felt this was just the type of challenge and occasion, at Lord's, to get Viv Richards going.

Richards? He didn't even get in. Greenidge batted magnificently for the first of his doubles that year, Gomes played as sensibly as usual and England's bowlers were all over the place. Greenidge relished their length and line that allowed him to cut to his heart's content. He finished unbeaten on 214 with a phenomenal number of boundaries, two sixes and 29 fours, Gomes was 92 and we won with 11.5 overs to spare, losing only one wicket, Haynes run out.

Greenidge's other double-century in the fourth Test at Old Trafford was completely different in character. We were in trouble at 70 for four and he guided us to calmer waters in big partnerships with Jeffrey Dujon, who got 101, and Winston Davis, who came in as night-watchman and made 77. We went on to total 500 and win by an innings and 64 runs.

Gordon was brought up in England and made his name there with Hampshire before returning to Barbados to bat his way into the West Indies team. He had to adjust to Caribbean conditions and Caribbean lifestyle before establishing himself and he never really overcame the feeling that he was an outsider. He and Viv Richards came into the team at the same time and went out at the same time and I believe his approach to the game was, in a large way, conditioned by the fact that he felt he did not get the acclaim Viv did in spite of his own outstanding record. He didn't have Viv's natural talent so he worked hard on his game by analysing his weaknesses, enhancing his best strokes, the cut and hook, and improving his fitness and his fielding. Even at the age of forty, he was able to bat for over eleven hours in the 1991 Barbados Test against Australia for his highest Test score, 226. By dint of his single-minded commitment, he developed one of the soundest techniques of any batsman of his time, which made him so good against all types of bowling in any conditions.

Gordon was a very private person, precise and meticulous in everything he did. He kept very much to himself which gave him a reputation of being moody and because of this he was certainly not the most popular cricketer around. It was some years, in fact, before he would take part in team discussions, but no-one could doubt his dedication to his profession or his important role in our long period of domination. Throughout his long career, he never batted better than he did at Lord's and Old Trafford in that summer of 1984.

By now, Clive Lloyd had cultivated such a remarkable spirit in the team that we never felt anything was beyond us and were never prepared to accept any cause as hopeless. This attitude repeatedly manifested itself during the series, never better than in the third Test at Leeds.

England totalled 270 in their first innings during which Malcolm Marshall broke his left thumb while fielding. It seemed certain he was out for the rest of the match, probably the series, a serious setback for us so early in the game. We were 18 ahead when our ninth wicket fell with Larry Gomes unbeaten on 96, an agonising shortfall for what was another sterling innings by the little left-hander. Suddenly, Clive asked Malcolm if he felt up to going out to see if he could stay long enough to let Larry reach the landmark. Malcolm hardly hesitated in his reply and, after a quick padding-up operation involving plenty of helpers, he scampered on to the field to the surprise of the England fielders and Larry himself, all of whom were starting to come off the field. Malcolm not only stayed to see Larry pass his century but also hit a one-handed boundary off Paul Allott before the innings ended. But the story didn't end there. Since his right, bowling hand, was perfectly fit Malcolm came back out to open the bowling and demolished England's second innings with controlled swing, taking seven for 53. For England to be destroyed by a one-hand man was the final, decisive blow to their self-esteem and they couldn't raise a fight after that.

As it was my last Test series in England, this was when I chose the last Test at The Oval for a little nostalgia by lengthening my run once more. Perhaps I was subconsciously trying to recreate the youthful joy of 1976. I was still enjoying my cricket and the continuing success of the West Indies and, even though I couldn't get away from the little injuries that kept recurring throughout my career, I looked forward to another tour of Australia within a couple of months.

It was the first full tour by the West Indies in the six seasons since the disbanding of World Series Cricket, and indeed the first with five Tests since 1975–76. It involved not only the Tests but also six matches against State teams, a few up-country games and thirteen one-dayers in the usual World Series Cup plus four more in the World Championship of Cricket stuck on at the end for some obscure reason. Even with that daunting schedule, lasting five months, I was enthusiastic about the tour. Australia by now was almost a second home to me, and there was a wonderful spirit in the team; also, since Clive Lloyd had announced it was to be his last series, there was an added incentive to do well.

CHAPTER 20

It's a tough game

When we arrived in Sydney in October for our 1984–85 tour, the Australians had had no cricket since their tour to the Caribbean earlier in the year and there was no noticeable change in their cricket. Before we went into the first Test, Kim Hughes was under pressure from almost all sections of the press and some eminent former players. There was also controversy over team selection.

It was a combination that virtually guaranteed failure. You only have to glance through the pages of cricket history to see how often results have been determined by events in the dressing-room or around the selection table. It was a failing we fully exploited earlier in the year against both Australia and England and we did so again.

The first Test was at the WACA in Perth, always my favourite ground. The pitch is magnificent for cricket, fast with even bounce and sure to last all five days. The sighting is good and everyone has a fair chance. It is ideal for bowling fast, possibly the reason we had not been given a Test there on our previous two tours, and Australia followed our lead in picking four fast bowlers. So we had Malcolm Marshall, Joel Garner, young Courtney Walsh and myself on our side, and Geoff Lawson, Carl Rackemann, Rodney Hogg and Terry Alderman on theirs. The atmosphere was electric in our dressing-room before the start as we were confident this was our ground and our Test.

It rained for two days before the match, we were sent in and were struggling at 104 for five and 186 for six. It took centuries of real class and character by Larry Gomes and Jeffrey Dujon to rebuild the innings. This was further proof of the spirit in the team, of the never-say-die attitude that we felt we did not get full credit for by those always keen to pull us down. Our main batsmen, Gordon Greenidge, Viv Richards and Clive Lloyd, were all out cheaply, both Gomes and Dujon were hit on the head early in their innings, yet we still piled up a total of 416.

That kind of fightback was an immediate psychological boost and we followed with what was one of the most brilliant periods of cricket in my Test experience. The ball kept flying off the edge and the catches kept sticking. Lloyd held one an inch from the ground at first slip. Dujon dived wide down the leg-side to catch Allan Border off my bowling. I fastened on to a slash from Kepler Wessels at gully and Marshall judged two perfectly down at long-leg from hook shots.

I went back to my long run and put everything I had into it. It wasn't quite The Oval 1976 but it was satisfying all the same to finish with six for 21 as Australia were toppled for 76, their lowest total in a Test against the West Indies. That was a crushing blow to their spirit and they folded to defeat by an innings and 112 runs.

The die had been cast in more ways than one. Even an emergency trip to the dressing-room by Lloyd during play helped yield a wicket. His business complete, he was waiting to rejoin play at the end of an over, so he watched the remaining deliveries on the dressing-room TV set. He came out, reported that he noticed Graham

Yallop wasn't moving into line and shifted Gordon Greenidge from fourth slip to square gully. Next ball, Yallop fended a catch straight to Greenidge. It's that way in cricket. When you're playing well, everything runs for you. The opposite is true, as that match also demonstrated.

Kim Hughes was an outgoing, friendly, down-to-earth individual. He was easy to get on with but seemed to have the habit of saying the wrong thing at the wrong time. When he forswore hooking at the pre-match press conference, he was tempting fate. He was a compulsive hooker and everyone knew it. I kept him waiting a little while after he came in before I let him have the inevitable bouncer. The bat went for it like a magnet, he didn't quite middle it and Marshall held a great catch above his head on the fence. Hughes played exactly the same shot with exactly the same result in the second Test at Brisbane, Marshall this time taking the catch off Garner.

The knives had been out for Kim for a long time and he gave those armed with them an excellent chance to sink them in. After we won the second Test by another big margin, eight wickets, he cracked under what he called 'the constant criticism, speculation and innuendo by former players'. He broke down in tears before the assembled TV cameras and international press, and announced his resignation as captain.

No-one likes to see a fellow sportsman so emotionally distraught but Test cricket is a rugged business and captains need to be mentally strong. Ever since Tony Greig's 'grovel' statement in England, we had made it a point to pay a little more attention to the captain of the opposing team and we certainly weren't going to ease up on Hughes. Why the Australian selectors then kept him in the side as a player following his resignation was a mystery. He was a broken man and he got three ducks in his next four innings before they finally left him out.

Allan Border stepped into the breach as the new captain while Hughes drifted out of the Test side only to resurface a year later as captain of the first Australian rebel side to South Africa.

Border was a much tougher character and has remained at the helm ever since. He had a difficult job trying to rebuild team spirit and he chose to take a more belligerent attitude to his opponents, on and off the field. I could sense the change as the Aussie boys suddenly became very aggressive and stand-offish. Australian cricket had gone through difficult times and I could understand Border's desire to turn things around but he went overboard. There was a lot of unnecessary antagonism and relations between the teams quickly deteriorated to reach a new low in the 1991 series in the Caribbean. It came home to me in the last Test in Sydney when Australia had their only victory, by an innings and 55 runs. The pitch broke up early and their spinners, Bob Holland and Murray Bennett, made the most of it. Yet I found Border, wearing spiked boots, walking right down the pitch between overs. I was surprised a captain should stoop to such tactics so I asked: 'What's that all about? You don't think the ball's turning enough already?' He snapped back: 'What's the matter? You can't take the heat now we're winning?' and continued his on-pitch strolling. In that same match, Border and wicket-keeper Steve Rixon got into a heated argument on the field with Viv Richards after an appeal against Richards. Such flare-ups between the teams became more and more commonplace, a real pity since the teams had enjoyed good personal relations over the years in spite of the keen competitiveness on the field.

When Border took over as captain, we were already

two up in the series and we extended our run of victories to a record eleven Tests by winning again in Adelaide, by 191 runs. There were confident predictions all round that we were heading for another clean sweep to follow the one over England a few months earlier, and it certainly would have been a grand way for Clive Lloyd to have ended his Test career. It didn't work out that way and we had ourselves to blame.

Richards emerged from a bad patch to score a double-century in the fourth Test at Melbourne and we were in a winning position by the close of the fourth day when we had an overall lead of 346. I had strained muscles in my side and missed that match and the preceding one at Adelaide but I was strongly in Clive's corner when the matter of an overnight declaration was discussed at the team meeting prior to the last day. We were 3–0 up in the series and a declaration was the obvious way to go but the players were split. So Clive, as he often did, put it to the vote and the decision was to bat on for a bit. It was a strangely defensive move by a usually attacking team and it cost us victory as Australia hung on grimly with eight wickets down at the end.

We then went straight to Sydney knowing full well what to expect. We were soundly beaten there for the only time on the tour in the State match against New South Wales when their spinners, Bob Holland, the leg-spinner, and Murray Bennett, the left-armer, ran through us on a pitch that turned square. They were there again waiting for us, this time in Test colours.

By now, I was fit again and there was a lot of hemming and hawing and prodding of the pitch before we decided on the final eleven. In the end, Roger Harper, the off-spinner, was left out so that I could return. It was an obviously wrong decision, given the known condition of the pitch, but I am sure Clive Lloyd made it

on sentiment. It was his last Test and who could blame
him if he wanted to go out with four fast bowlers, the
policy he had devised and so successfully carried out.
The Australians picked the bowling to suit the pitch
and we went down to our first defeat in a Test since
we lost at Melbourne three years earlier. Clive himself
put up a brave fight to save us in the second innings
with a high-class 72 but it was in vain. We could only
total 163 and 253 in our two innings and were thrashed
by an innings and 55 runs.

As he left the ground to an emotional standing
ovation from a crowd of over 20,000, Clive Lloyd
knew he would bow out in defeat. It must have been
a real let-down for him but he took it philosophically
and there was a little consolation as we then created
another record by winning all ten of our preliminary
round matches in the World Series Cup with Australia
and Sri Lanka before securing the Cup again 2–1 in the
final against Australia. I was back to full fitness, played
in eleven of the twelve matches and had the satisfaction of taking five wickets in the third and decisive
final.

By then, the season had dragged on long enough.
We had been in Australia four months but there was still
the business of what the organisers called 'The Greatest
Show on Turf' to complete. It was a limited-overs tournament between all seven Test countries organised as
a celebration of Victoria's 150th anniversary as a State.
Really, it was to inaugurate the lights at the Melbourne
Cricket Ground and a chance finally to upstage Sydney which had already had its lights in place for seven
years. We played like the tired team we were and the
tournament ended for us in the semi-final when we
batted poorly to be all out for 159 and lost by seven
wickets to Pakistan.

It was another closing disappointment for Clive

Lloyd in what was his last match for the West Indies. An era in West Indies cricket was at an end.

CHAPTER 21

Life after Lloyd

Clive Lloyd's was a hard act to follow. He had led the West Indies since 1974, a span broken only briefly by the Packer years, had a record as Test captain that bore no comparison, and retired when he and his team were still on top. To me, and I am sure most of those who played under him, he was not only a great cricketer but someone we knew always put the interest of his team and his players above everything else. He was loyal to us and we to him.

He left to a stream of flattering tributes, including the award of the Order of Australia, the country's highest honour, rarely given to non-nationals. Weaker, less experienced teams might have been shaken by the departure of someone of his calibre, but we were able to make the transition with little disruption. Viv Richards had been Clive's deputy since Deryck Murray's exit in 1981 and moved naturally into the position after a long wait. Though his style of leadership was as different as their personalities, the stalwarts who had been with Clive for most of his time – Greenidge, Haynes, Garner and myself – were still there and the team remained powerful and settled.

The New Zealanders came on what was only their second tour of the Caribbean as soon as we got back from Australia in March 1985 and were our first assignment under Viv Richards. They didn't provide much of a challenge and neither did England a year later. We were winning as repeatedly and as comfortably as we had under Clive and a few newer players were settling themselves into the team, an essential development.

Richie Richardson showed his potential with a couple of big centuries against Australia in the West Indies early in 1984, got another century in Australia in the Test in Brisbane and clinched the spot with an innings of 185 in the second Test against the New Zealanders in Guyana. Gus Logie, who had been in the reserves for several tours, took Lloyd's place in the middle order, a big responsibility for a little man, and Courtney Walsh had already made his first appearance in the fast quartet. I was particularly pleased with Walsh's progress as he was a Melbourne man and I played with him when he first came into the club as a highly promising junior on leaving school.

The series against New Zealand was the first between the teams since our contentious series there five years earlier and, happily, there were no repercussions. It gave West Indian crowds the chance to see Richard Hadlee, their one truly great player, but they never got into the series at all as we won the last two Tests with ease after the first two were drawn. More than anyone else, Hadlee gained international respect for New Zealand cricket by his magnificent achievements for which he was knighted after he retired in 1990. He did not do it entirely on his own and he was not quite at his best on the West Indies tour but I wonder where New Zealand would have been without his bowling and his uplifting influence for so long. Throughout his long career, he was their one and only strike bowler. His main assets were his rhythm and his classically smooth action, both the basis of control. He didn't bowl many no-balls and never looked to be struggling. On pitches with a little grass, such as those in England and New

Zealand, he readily exploited any flaws in batting technique. He knew exactly what he wanted to do and how to do it, moving the ball around, especially away from the bat.

He was also a dangerous left-handed batsman low in the order who played some vital innings for New Zealand and hit a century off us at Christchurch in the 1980 series. You wouldn't call him the bravest batsman in the world and he wasn't keen to get into line against the fast bowlers. But he was a powerful hitter who was only concerned with making runs, not how he looked.

New Zealand built up a good, solid side in the 1980s but had to rely too heavily on too few players. It seemed to me they placed too much emphasis on their record of not losing a series at home for twelve years which, if they were honest with themselves, was based to a large extent on the peculiar interpretation of the laws by their umpires. It gave them a false sense of security and their limitations tended to be exposed away from home. This was the case in the Caribbean, even though they were never less than competitive.

Injury again curtailed my series, a recurrence of the strained rib-cage muscles from Australia forcing me to miss the final Test at home at Sabina Park. But I was fit enough to return to Derbyshire for the start of the 1985 county season.

A sequence of events had limited my appearances since I had signed for them and I looked forward now to an uninterrupted season. After the 1983 final at Lord's, I got caught in the crowd as I ran back to the pavilion and someone trampled my foot so badly it tore ligaments and delayed my Derbyshire debut until the middle of August. The following year, I was on tour with the West Indies.

So I was making a belated debut for my county. My contract was for twelve championship matches plus all the one-dayers and I managed to honour it fully over the next five enjoyable seasons I spent at Derby before playing my last first-class match in 1989.

The Australians were in England for another Ashes series during that 1985 summer and, having just played them in Australia and with England scheduled to tour the West Indies the following season, I was interested in the contest. When England won the last two Tests by an innings to take the series 3–1 and regain the Ashes, they were optimistic about their chances in the Caribbean. Instead, they suffered another humiliating defeat.

There was more to the series than cricket. Several of those who had been on the rebel tour to South Africa just three years earlier had served their bans and returned to the England team for the tour, among them Graham Gooch, who had been their captain. Guyana was again off-limits but the remaining governments decided they could come under the terms of the Gleneagles Agreement. I was not entirely happy myself that the length of the ban on England's rebel players was long enough but whether the tour should proceed was a political decision. I understood the rationale for the governments' decision but I don't think the political leaders were prepared for the intensity of feeling of those opposed to the tour and the Tests were subjected to strong protest demonstrations and crowd boycotts, especially in Trinidad. The issue emphasised that cricket could not be isolated from the issues of the day and, in this case, one so close to the hearts of the people.

The furore may have had some effect on the England side but not half as much as the pitch they encountered in the first one-day international and the first Test at Sabina Park. I was Jamaica captain for the first time that season and we fielded a strong pace attack. In addition to Courtney Walsh and myself, we had Patrick Patterson and Aaron Daley, a strong policeman who bowled stiff fast-medium. Patterson had been in and out of the Jamaica team a few years earlier and impressed Clive Lloyd so much during a net session that he took him off to play for Lancashire in the county championship and then arranged a contract for him in Tasmania. He was big, strong and very fast but bowled too short in England and had problems with stamina. He was virtually unheard-of in the West Indies when the season started but came back home to get into the Jamaica team. He worked very hard on his fitness and his bowling and was soon a sensation. At Sabina, he was a menace.

Jamaicans used to boast that Sabina had one of the best pitches anywhere. I've seen pictures with the players' images reflecting from it like a mirror in the days when it was very fast and bouncy but also very true. In the late 1960s, the ground authorities dug it up and relaid it. They kept turning it over every year so that you weren't sure how it was going to play from season to season, even week to week. That year it was frightening. It was fast but the bounce was completely unpredictable. One ball would skid through to hit you on the ankles, the next would fly over the 'keeper's head and go for four byes, something which happened several times.

In our first Shell Shield match, Guyana were bowled out for 41 and Patterson took seven for 24. Walsh had eight in the second innings. In the next match the Leewards, with Viv Richards and Richie Richardson in their order, could only muster 77 and their opener, Luther Kelly, had to be taken off, spitting out a couple of teeth when he was hit in the mouth by one from Patterson that flew.

It was a portent of things to come. England won the island match against Jamaica but, even though

Patterson was being held back as the West Indies surprise weapon, the signs were there as Walsh and Daley gave them a torrid time. Both Allan Lamb and David Gower were hit on the helmet. That was more than enough to make them apprehensive and their worst fears were realised in the first one-day international a few days later. Mike Gatting, hooking at Malcolm Marshall, missed and took a terrible blow that completely shattered his nose. It is a sickening feeling to see anyone injured at any time but more so in sport and Gatting's bloodied and flattened nose bridge was a shocking sight as he left the field. Marshall and Joel Garner said afterwards they found a small piece of bone lodged in the seam of the ball when they picked it up. It was an incident that added fuel to the fire being stoked against our fast bowlers and our tactics. The truth is that no fast bowler should carry the blame for pitches that are completely unsuitable for the game at the highest level.

Gatting is a gutsy character, a real British bull-dog, and he returned later in the tour after going back to England for an operation. But that incident and more fearsome bowling from Patterson, Marshall and Garner in the Test totally undermined whatever self-confidence and optimism England might have had. By the final Test in Antigua, when Richards slammed the fastest century in Test history off 56 balls with six sixes and seven fours, the crowd was singing the hit calypso of the time, 'Captain, the ship is sinking', as England slid to another 5–0 'blackwash'.

A lot was made in the English press of the laid-back attitude of the captain, David Gower, and some key members of the team. Allegations about Ian Botham's nocturnal activities with a certain Barbadian beauty queen got a lot of play in the tabloids. A lack of commitment might have been a reason for the crushing defeat and the anti-tour campaign might have been another. But nothing was as significant as the jolt they got from their first encounter with our fast bowling on that devil of a pitch at Sabina Park.

Gower lost the captaincy after that tour, just as Botham lost it after the previous series in the Caribbean five years earlier, but there wasn't much either could have done to change things. Gower, in fact, was England's leading batsman in a series in which they did not score a single century.

CHAPTER 22

The end of the road

I had been considering my future in Test cricket for some time before the home series against England in 1986 and intimated as much to the selectors more than once. Each time, both Clyde Walcott and Jackie Hendriks persuaded me that I still had a few years left and that I was needed. Now my mind was made up. Injuries seemed more persistent than ever, I wasn't performing to my own satisfaction and there were several young fast bowlers waiting in the wings. Courtney Walsh had to take a back seat when Patterson made his dramatic entrance and Tony Gray and Winston Benjamin were just coming on to the scene. They were in their early twenties and had everywhere to go. The replacements were there. It was time to call it a day.

Again, Hendriks intervened with his powers of persuasion. A tour of Pakistan was to follow, starting in October 1986, and he felt that Joel Garner and I, the only two of the original quartet remaining, needed a rest from international cricket. So he proposed leaving us out of that tour if we would return for the trip to Australia and New Zealand to follow immediately. He was bargaining and, while I would not have gone to the Board and asked for a rest, if he was offering, I would accept.

On reflection, it was a mistake. After another satisfying season with Derbyshire, I remained in Jamaica and didn't get very much training. I was jaded and needed the break. When we left for Australia in December to take part in a one-day series before going on to New Zealand, I knew I wasn't as fit as I should have been.

We arrived in Perth to join the Perth Challenge Series that was tied in with Australia's yachting defence of the America's Cup and I headed down to the large open park down by the Swan River around dawn to start my training. I had always done my running there when in Perth but I now found it a chore. It was symptomatic of what followed on that tour.

By some bureaucratic bungle, we flew to Australia through Christmas Eve night and arrived in Perth Christmas morning. It was not an auspicious start especially since we discovered that the captain, Viv Richards, had been given permission by the Board to spend Christmas at home before flying out. Things went from bad to worse after that. Team morale was low, we had problems with injuries, some real, some imagined, there was bickering between players and we lost match after match.

Our difficulties concerned one of our senior players in particular, Gordon Greenidge. He had a reputation for overreacting to injuries and it was almost a standing joke among players that once he started to limp, look out, he was bound to score runs. Back in Australia in 1981–82, Clive Lloyd had to give him an ultimatum – to play or to go home – to get him back in the Test team after some knee injury kept him out. He decided to play and scored a brilliant half-century, still limping of course. Now, our batting was struggling and, without his class and experience as opener, we weren't getting the starts we were accustomed to. We needed him back badly but no-one could cajole him successfully. Gus Logie, who was sharing a room with him, tried but said Gordon told him it was time he had a rest after doing the hard work for so many years. Not that his knee was still too painful or that he couldn't manage it but that he wanted a rest. He said in a radio interview he felt stale. With so much cricket, it is a condition that affects most international cricketers at some time but it took an untimely moment to overcome Gordon. Not surprisingly, a lot of mutual antagonism developed between him and the rest of the team.

We came to the last game in the preliminary round of the World Series Cup against England in Devonport, in Tasmania, needing to win to qualify for the finals. We had won the Cup every time we had contested it and were keen to maintain our record. We had another setback when Desmond Haynes dislocated his finger at fielding practice the day before and Viv, myself and the manager, Stephen Camacho, tried again to get Greenidge to play, even if he wasn't one hundred per cent fit. But he wouldn't budge, so we picked the eleven overnight without him, using Thelston Payne, the reserve wicketkeeper, to open with Richie Richardson. Next morning, Greenidge announced he was willing to play after all but Viv had had enough by then and decided to go into the match without him. We were bowled out for 148, lost again, failed to make the finals and headed for New Zealand.

Our decline was a big story in Australia. They had become accustomed to the West Indies winning everything in sight and, since this was our first appearance there with Viv as captain, he got a lot of the blame. But the problems were not his fault. It was one-day cricket, in which you don't have a chance to come back after a bad batting performance, and the batting let us down badly. There is nothing a captain can do about that. Some players tried to blame the change in conditions from Pakistan to Australia but the answer was that we started to lose and, with Greenidge's absence and a few key injuries, we couldn't pick back up. When that happens in Australia, players try to get their minds off the cricket by turning their attention to the many comforts of life that are offered there. There was a snowball effect as things went from bad to worse.

The tour selectors, Viv, manager Camacho and myself, had to assess our many injuries and determine, in particular, whether we should take Greenidge to New Zealand where we had three Tests, two first-class matches and four one-day internationals at the end of the six weeks. We were all agreed at that stage that, great player that he was, we could not carry him. I left the meeting under the impression that we would ask for a replacement. As it turned out, Greenidge did come to New Zealand with us and proceeded to make a packet of runs, including a double-century in the second Test at Auckland and single centuries in two of the one-day internationals.

I'm still unclear as to what exactly caused the switch but the captain did tell the press that Gordon was too good a player to leave out. I believe Viv was nervous about the team's batting and felt that Gordon's injury would disappear as soon as the Tests started.

By now, I was completely fed up with everything – unhappy with the general behaviour of the team, the spirit, my own performance and my fitness after I pulled a hamstring diving for a return catch off Ian Botham in Melbourne. There was squabbling on petty matters between some senior members that almost came to blows on occasion and cliques started to develop. Nothing was going right and I wanted out. It took me back to my very first tour eleven years earlier and, even though I was now in a position of authority as vice-captain, I felt powerless to do anything to change it. When I developed a back problem in the first Test in New Zealand, I asked

Stephen Camacho to arrange a ticket for me to leave since my tour, and my Test career, were at an end. Like Jackie Hendriks earlier, Camacho asked me to think it over. The time for thinking over had long passed and I left for home on the day the second Test began in Auckland.

When I got back to Jamaica, an immigration officer at Norman Manley Airport pointed out that I needed one more wicket for my 250th in Tests but that didn't mean a thing to me. Nor did another piece of trivia which I heard in the radio commentary relayed back from New Zealand later in the series. It was that I had taken the same number of wickets in my final Test as in my first – none!

After nearly a dozen years in Test cricket, most of them happy and successful, perhaps I should have been more emotional or chosen a more auspicious moment to take my leave. Instead, I was overcome by neither sadness nor regret, only relief.

There was even controversy over who would take over the vice-captaincy. When Viv Richards succeeded Clive Lloyd as skipper, I was appointed his deputy. The selectors knew I got on well with Viv and probably felt we would make a good combination for it certainly wasn't a matter of grooming me as a future captain. When I took a rest on the tour of Pakistan, Malcolm Marshall was named vice-captain which certainly seemed a pointer to the future. I didn't expect to be reinstated on my return and, when I was, Malcolm was understandably miffed. They turned to him again on my return home from New Zealand but he said he was no yo-yo to be used by the Board and pointedly declined. Within a few months, Joel Garner and Larry Gomes announced their retirements as well while Marshall and Greenidge pulled out from the World Cup in India and Pakistan the following October.

I am sure these were decisions all prompted by events in Australia and New Zealand.

I was sorry that Viv had to confront such upheavals so early in his captaincy. He had taken over after a long wait as Clive Lloyd's deputy and, as there had been a lot of doubts about his temperament and his capacity to handle the job, he desperately wanted to make a success of it. He was a very proud man to whom the team's reputation, and his own, were very important. It was an intensity he transmitted to those under him but, as captain, he was often his own worst enemy.

He had played the game for a long time and always read it well. His problem centred around his dealings with people, an important part of leadership and one in which Clive Lloyd earned full marks. Off the field, Viv was a reasonable, personable individual but it was a different matter out in the middle. Once involved in the game, he would get so intensely involved he could lose his cool very easily, as I saw several times in his career, both as player and as captain. I know he tried hard to temper himself but he was, by nature, emotional and volatile. Had he been any different, I don't believe he would have been the dominant, super-confident batsman he was, but they were not ideal characteristics for captaincy.

Viv certainly had no challengers as Lloyd's successor. No-one in the team stood out as potentially a better skipper. He was a strong character who set high standards of performance for his players, precisely because he was so fiercely conscious of what success meant for the West Indies and West Indian people. The upshot was that he came down hard on those who fell short of his expectations. His players didn't seem to warm to him and I detected in his latter years that individuals were playing more for themselves than for the captain. Man-management calls for tact, patience and understanding but these did not come easily for such a passionate man as Viv Richards.

CHAPTER 23

The international professional

For one who had no initial ambitions to become a professional cricketer, I ended up as quite an international freelancer. I was twenty-seven and had already played twenty-eight Tests before I took up my first contract in English league cricket, and I was thirty-one in my first full season in the county championship. Yet I stayed five and a half seasons with Derbyshire and a season each with Tasmania in Australia and with Canterbury in New Zealand. Adding my several tours with the West Indies, I physically spent more than half my fourteen years in international cricket outside of Jamaica and played almost twice as many matches for Derbyshire as for Jamaica, 66 against 34.

My first professional assignment outside West Indies was with Kerry Packer's WSC, which changed not only the game as a whole but the course of my life. I am positive I would not have taken it up full-time had Packer's intervention not so transformed pay as to make it worthwhile employment. I am also positive I would have sought some other occupation had the only avenue available been the Lancashire League.

I grew up hearing about league cricket since that was the only professional outlet for West Indians before the county circuit opened up in the 1960s. Yet I didn't know what to expect when I signed for Rishton in 1981 and I do not mean to be derisive when I say I soon discovered I went at the wrong stage of my career. The league is suited to three types of cricketer – the youngster at the start of his career seeking the experience of different conditions, the former Test player wanting to see out his days as a professional, and the solid all-rounder not quite good enough to have made it at the highest level. At the time I didn't fit into any of those categories.

The Rishton team comprised amateurs. While there were a few fair players, the overall standard was nowhere near that of club cricket in Jamaica. In any league club, the pro is the be-all-and-end-all of the team, expected to get the wickets and make the runs, and it is a great exercise for an up-and-coming young player. Dozens and dozens from every country, mainly the West Indies, have benefited from it even though the leagues no longer get the cream of the crop as they used to do.

My problem was lack of motivation. I'd come off playing Packer cricket, Tests and Shell Shield, the highest, most competitive levels of the game, and I couldn't make the necessary adjustment. Nor did an extraordinarily wet summer with damp pitches improve my impression. The social atmosphere at the club was very friendly and the people most warm and generous but it was not the type of cricket I was looking for.

The county scene was altogether different. Everyone was professional and expected to perform consistently at a particular level and some of the best players in the world were on the circuit. In my time, first briefly with Lancashire and then with Derbyshire, I was, therefore, surprised and disappointed with the attitude of a great majority of English players. They seemed to see county cricket as no more than a comfortable living and were not interested in moving up to a higher level, to play Test cricket for their country.

The general outlook was that if the call came from the England selectors, all well and good, but very few seemed willing to put in the extra effort to make sure it did happen, to run the extra mile at training, to spend the extra hour in the nets to achieve that standard. County cricket provides a reasonable living, even for the ordinary player who would get his 1,000 runs or his 40 or 50 wickets a season. He gets his sponsored car and other perks, has his expenses paid, 'works' outdoors in the summer sun (well, when it's shining!) and enjoys a relaxed, sociable environment. Most appeared satisfied with that, knowing that if they stayed around long enough they could look forward to a healthy, tax-free benefit on retirement that would take care of their future.

The attitude seemed to be, why bust a gut trying to make the Test team where the pay isn't that much better and where the pressure is intense? It's such an attractive life that several county players come out of university and choose cricket rather than earning a little more money stuck behind a desk, knowing they have a degree to fall back on in the end.

Coming from the West Indies, and then playing in Australia and New Zealand, it struck me as a strange lack of ambition. The explanation, I believe, has to do with the professional structure. Everywhere else, only Test cricket offers good pay, so there is fierce competition in the Red Stripe Cup or the Sheffield Shield to win Test places and to retain them. In England, the pay differential is not that great, so Test selection doesn't provide much of a financial incentive.

During my time at Derbyshire, a young batsman I considered one of the most talented in England,

John Morris, was an example of this syndrome. It had become almost endemic and John seems to have let his chance slip by. He was finally recognised by the England selectors for their tour of Australia in 1990–91 but he didn't hold on to his place and sometimes I wonder if he put in the necessary work.

It is true that there is no more physically demanding cricket in the world than in England and this is another reason why the players don't put in one hundred per cent effort all the time. It is too tough to maintain fitness and, more important, enthusiasm for an entire season from mid-April through to mid-September. The regular county pro plays something like twenty first-class matches and twenty one-day matches a season, logging up thousands of miles on the motorways travelling from ground to ground. It is no wonder the dozens of ordinary players, with no prospects of a place on the England team and in teams with no chance at any title, lose interest and go through the motions for half the season. In both Lancashire and Derbyshire dressing-rooms, I often heard a sigh of relief when rain washed out cricket. It was considered a day off. I could understand it because I was doing the same thing myself in the end. Then, I knew it was time to get out.

England went through rough times in the 1980s and all sorts of reasons were advanced, excuses given and remedies put forward. For all the blame placed on overseas players, bad pitches, lack of discipline, poor coaching and whatever else, the truth was that there was a dearth of really talented cricketers. In my final year at Derbyshire in 1989, there was no-one in England I could point to and say he would go on to score 5,000 Test runs or take 200 wickets – as you could with David Gower, Ian Botham and Graham Gooch a dozen years earlier. And I'm purposely not including in that list the off-shore Englishmen like Robin Smith or Graeme Hick who qualified either by family relationships or residence.

Worried by this, the authorities have shown a certain panic in the measures introduced to counteract the decline. The bonus points system has not served any purpose, except to encourage defensive bowling and slogging by the middle-order batsmen. The limitation to one overseas player per county will simply reduce the number of world-class players and diminish the standard.

In my later years, the main debate concerned the structure of the championship and whether four-day matches are the answer. The Test and County Cricket Board (TCCB) set up a committee to consider the issue. This has finally recommended seventeen four-day matches for each county, doing away with the three-day matches that were the basis of English cricket for more than a hundred years. I agree with the four-day idea but, from my experience, I doubt whether the majority of pitches can last that long. Whether it was the way they were prepared or whether it had to do with the soil I don't know, but I found most championship pitches broke up by the third day.

If the groundsmen can now make pitches that will last, the new format should be beneficial. Batsmen will have time to build their innings, instead of chasing runs for bonus points, and bowlers will have to learn to get batsmen out rather than waiting for the opposition to declare to make a match of it, as happened so often in three-day matches.

Above all, I believe the county match programme needs to be reduced to give players the chance to recharge their batteries, even to practise. It is obvious one-day matches are essential as money-spinners, but

I'm sure a reduction would make the players happier, and better.

I had my first contact with county cricket with Lancashire during my 1981 stint with Rishton. My longer association came a few years later with Derbyshire. I was in Tasmania on another contract for the 1982–83 season when Geoff Miller approached me during our match against the touring England team and asked if I was interested in coming into county cricket. I'd got no offers before then as I'm sure the word was out that the prospect of daily cricket didn't appeal to me and I repeated my position to Geoff. However, I had not been satisfied with league cricket and I started to take interest when Geoff mentioned the possibility of a limited contract.

An agreement was worked out through Jack Simmons that appealed to me. I would play half the championship matches plus all the one-dayers. Jack was the Lancashire all-rounder who, along with Clive Lloyd, had a placement agency for professional cricketers and had finalised my terms with Rishton and with Tasmania. Not that it was as cut and dried as that. The issue of overseas players had become a topic of debate by then and, even though I was being signed on because John Wright would be on tour with the New Zealand team, Derbyshire had to satisfy the TCCB that I would play for them for at least two seasons. By the time I'd had my first full season, the regulation limited the counties to one overseas player per match, so I alternated with Wright.

The Derbyshire sojourn, and county cricket as a whole, was most pleasant. My one regret was that we didn't win anything in my five seasons. Our highest position in the championship was sixth in 1986 and when we did get to the final of one of the one-day competitions, the Benson & Hedges Cup, in 1988, we blew it. Hampshire were our opponents and, even though they were without Malcolm Marshall, who was touring with the West Indies, we were beaten from the time we lost four early wickets to Stephen Jeffries, a left-arm South African who bowled big, late inswingers. We lost the toss, always a disadvantage with an early start at Lord's, I was in and out before lunch, caught at long-off, and we couldn't possibly defend a total of 117. It was my first final at Lord's since the 1983 World Cup and another disappointment.

I left Derbyshire with several pleasant memories and a host of friends although the performance that attracted most attention during my final season in 1989 had nothing to do with my bowling. It occurred at Trent Bridge in our match against Nottinghamshire and, while I thought I had seen just about everything in cricket, this took the cake!

The pitches had become a major issue with justified accusations that certain counties prepared them – or, to be more accurate, underprepared them – to ensure outright results and more points. This was undoubtedly the case in the match in question. It was, simply, the worst pitch I have ever played on. The ball exploded off it and on the first day, the Saturday, twenty wickets fell. We had a Sunday league match at Edgbaston the following day and when we resumed on the Monday, it was obvious things had reached a stage where it was no longer playable. After he was caught at short-leg off a particularly nasty flier from me, Chris Broad, the Notts' opener, shook hands with the fielder, Martin Jean-Jacques, and said 'thanks'. At that point, the two captains, Kim Barnett of Derbyshire and Tim Robinson of Notts, agreed that conditions were unfit for play. Confronted with this reality, the umpires, Barry Meyer and Peter Wight, should have abandoned the match but they decided instead to seek guidance on the phone from the TCCB at Lord's.

If you know your geography, you'll know that St John's Wood is nearly two hundred miles away from Trent Bridge and what the TCCB officials could have known about conditions from that distance was beyond me. In their wisdom, they directed the umpires to continue the match on the adjacent pitch that had been used for the Test against Australia a week earlier. I felt someone had to take a stand against such nonsense and I informed Kim Barnett that I would not continue playing under such circumstances. So even though the match resumed, I took no further part. I was 'severely reprimanded' by the county but I suspect there were those on the committee who saw my point.

Before I left Derby, I was happy that Devon Malcolm had been rewarded for his persistence by inclusion in the England team and that I could have some influence on Ian Bishop joining the county. Malcolm is a fellow Jamaican and a genuine fast bowler and I took a special interest in him. He is one player who worked hard and committed himself to his improvement for he is not the natural that Bishop is. Now that Bishop has overcome the back problem that kept him out of the game for almost a year, they should be a formidable pair in years to come for Derbyshire.

My stints with Tasmania and Canterbury were altogether shorter but very enjoyable and rewarding. The format of the first-class game in both Australia and New Zealand is very different from that in England and very similar to the West Indies. There are six teams in each, compared with eighteen in England, so that the available talent is more concentrated, not diluted as I found it to be in England. It meant that very few ordinary players made the grade. Everyone was either a Test player or a potential Test player striving to reach the highest level. The competition was always intense and the cricket keen as a result.

In my first match for Tasmania, nine of the New South Wales eleven had either played or eventually played Test cricket for Australia, so it was a special feeling when we won. The same holds true in the Caribbean where Barbados, at one time, could put eleven Test players in their team. The Leeward Islands in the past couple of years have included Viv Richards, Richie Richardson, Curtly Ambrose, Keith Arthurton, Eldine Baptiste, Winston Benjamin, Kenneth Benjamin and Hamesh Anthony, all West Indies players. George Ferris and Tony Merrick, who played with English counties, couldn't even make the side. We've not had quite the same depth in Jamaica but when I first got into the team in 1973 it included five Test men and, as I noted earlier, I have shared a Jamaica attack with Courtney Walsh and Patrick Patterson.

Since my season with Tasmania coincided with their full entry into the Shield, it was a challenge for me to do well and I felt satisfied with my 36 wickets at the end and happy I'd had the experience.

Time is a great healer and my return to New Zealand, to play for Canterbury, came eight years after my first troubled visit there in 1980 when I left with such a bitter taste in my mouth. The West Indies returned in 1987 but I stayed only a few weeks before my decision to retire from Test cricket brought my tour to an end.

The invitation to join Canterbury for the 1988 season came from John Wright but I wasn't inclined to accept. 'Wrighty' had become a close friend over the years at Derbyshire but I really wasn't looking for more cricket straight after a tiring county stint. I was under the impression the New Zealand season coincided with Australia's, starting in October. When he explained the first match was not until after Christmas and I knew

I would have three months at home in the interim, I took him up on it. I phoned Bryan Adams of the Canterbury Association in Christchurch to talk terms and, as they were better even than Derbyshire's and for only eight four-day matches and three or four one-dayers, I quickly confirmed acceptance.

I was happy I did. For one, I found out that all New Zealand umpires are not cheats, a firm conviction we all had after 1980. I am still certain that some of the decisions then were downright biased but what I saw at their domestic level showed the problem to be more one of poor overall standards. The players only aggravated the situation by putting pressure on the umpires with concerted appeals. Ironically, the first wicket I got for Canterbury came from a bad decision. We were playing against the touring Queensland side from Australia when, to my surprise, everybody went up for an appeal for a catch at the wicket. I knew the ball hadn't gone anywhere near the bat but had come off the batsman's hip. All the same, up went the umpire's finger.

The cricket wasn't of an exceptionally high standard since the best players were with the New Zealand Test team in Australia at the time but it was hard-fought with the players fired by the incentive of Test selection. The weather and the pitches tended to be similar to those in England and I finished top of the bowling averages. The presence of Graeme Hick for Northern Districts gave a lift to the competition and we were on the receiving end of one of his four hundreds for the season. There were one or two up-and-coming New Zealand players who caught the eye. The first time I bowled to Mark Greatbatch he got 149 for Central Districts and looked a well-organised left-hander with sound technique. When I commented in the dressing-room that he was a definite Test prospect, I was told he was cocky and unpopular but it's interesting to see how well he's done since getting into the New Zealand Test side, especially his exploits in the 1992 World Cup. There were a few other good players around but New Zealand cricket will continue to suffer if it doesn't bring its umpiring up to standard.

I was near the end of my career but it was a new experience and I felt the enthusiasm of a first-timer. I was always conscious of not doing anything to give my fellow professionals, especially fellow West Indians, a bad name by not pulling my weight. I've heard it said often enough that so-and-so is only here because of his name and is collecting his fee without giving value. Especially at a time when there is so much critical comment about West Indian cricket, our pros need to guard our reputation carefully.

For all my seasons overseas, nothing could equal the atmosphere and the competitiveness of the Red Stripe Cup – or, as it used to be, the Shell Shield – in the West Indies. The rivalry was intense, the teams invariably strong, the crowds noisy and partisan. In England, it is county against county, in Australia state against state, in New Zealand province against province. In the West Indies, it is nation against nation and passions run high. In one of his books, Learie Constantine said he knew certain players in the Trinidad team carried revolvers for protection when they went to play in Guyana back in the 1920s. Though things aren't so lawless these days, controversy is never far from the surface. I've heard as great a player as Malcolm Marshall unmercifully booed and heckled by the Jamaican crowd at Sabina Park when he was Barbados' captain because he publicly accused the Jamaican umpires of cheating. And because umpires are selected from the home territory and many are inexperienced, we get the same problems that bother New Zealand cricket, and Test cricket.

Because of the distances between the territories, the

expenses for staging the tournament, such as air travel and accommodation in a pricey tourist area, are high. Balanced against that, the populations and the economies are small. There isn't much money around, so the West Indies Board limits the season to one round of five matches per team. More matches would obviously mean more exposure and more exposure would be better for the younger players. The Board claims that, even with sponsorship, a return round isn't feasible but I wonder if it has made enough effort for increased sponsorship.

The problem facing most domestic tournaments now is how to blend them in with the increasing demands of the international circuit. The West Indies season corresponds more or less with those in Australia and New Zealand so that, when our Test team is touring those countries, the Red Stripe Cup has to do without the leading players. Now that South Africa is back in world cricket, the issue is compounded. This diminishes standards and public interest just as it does in Australia where the Sheffield Shield has to share billing with the Tests and the World Series Cup. The West Indies Board insists that anyone who wishes to qualify for Test selection must play in the Red Stripe Cup, a ruling aimed at keeping our top players at home rather than taking up conflicting contracts elsewhere.

When at full strength, there is no more powerful domestic cricket than in the West Indies. In my first season, in 1973, aged nineteen, I had to bowl to a Guyana batting order of Roy Fredericks, Stephen Camacho, Len Baichan, Alvin Kallicharran, Clive Lloyd and Rohan Kanhai on one of the flattest pitches in the game at the Bourda ground in Georgetown. In the 1980s, opponents would have to face up to a Barbados attack of Malcolm Marshall, Joel Garner, Sylvester Clarke and Wayne Daniel. That kind of opposition separates the wheat from the chaff and is the foundation on which our consistency at Test level is built.

Overseas contracts, the Packer years and injury restricted my involvement but I did get the opportunity of leading the Jamaican team for two seasons, in 1986 and 1987, and was in the teams that won the Red Stripe Cup in its first two years, 1988 and 1989. Jamaica had gone twenty-one years without winning the championship when we pulled it off, under the captaincy of Marlon Tucker, in 1988.

Since it was the first year for the new sponsors whose product is advertised as 'the great Jamaican beer', it seemed appropriate. The Jamaican public, for so long starved of success, was ecstatic and one of my happiest memories will always be the team's triumphant round-the-island tour. It was a kind of lap of honour that lasted a weekend and seemed to stop at every town and village so the people could show us just how happy they were we had won it. It was the kind of reception the FA Cup winners in England get when they return home, only a dozen times over. There was a great spirit in the team and we repeated it the following season which was to be my last in the West Indies.

The last match in 1989 was to be the Cup decider, against Barbados at Kensington Oval, and we got the draw we needed to secure the championship. It was my final first-class appearance in the West Indies and I went out, not with a bang but with a whimper, caught at mid-on off Desmond Haynes who hardly ever bowls. Perhaps it wasn't so much a whimper as a snigger as Desmond and the others couldn't restrain their laughter as I headed back to the pavilion at Kensington for the last time.

CHAPTER 24

Changes – for better and worse

I played my cricket in changing, almost revolutionary times. If I had been born fifteen years earlier, I would not be able to sit with my grandchildren in my old age and tell them about the night at VFL Park in Melbourne that I was part of the first international match ever played under lights. I wouldn't have represented two counties in England, a state in Australia and a province in New Zealand. I wouldn't have played in a one-day international, far less a World Cup. I certainly wouldn't have been a professional cricketer.

It took the intervention of a private entrepreneur, Kerry Packer, fully backed by the leading players of the day, to initiate fundamental change when those who ran cricket could not recognise the need for it. Most of the innovations have proved beneficial – and not simply the increased pay that brought cricketers nearer parity with other professional international sportsmen. More money has come into the game as a whole through sponsorship, television has paid it more attention since the new techniques introduced by Packer's Channel Nine network, and it is spreading to such non-cricket locations as Sharjah, Toronto and New York.

Not all the changes have necessarily been for the better. The growth of the one-day game has affected overall standards by rewarding negative bowling and unorthodox batting. It is exciting, appeals to spectators and is here to stay but some account must be taken of its effects on the game as a whole. It is more than just coincidence that the country that went into rapid decline in the 1980s, England, plays more limited-overs cricket, and more varieties of it, than any other.

The experienced player, schooled in the basics of building an innings and bowling to get the batsman out, can adjust to one-day cricket with no side-effects. Those raised on it acquire bad habits that are hard to shake off, such as hitting across the line of the ball and bowling not to attack but to defend.

I am not condemning one-day cricket out of hand. Far from it. As I have already said, I enjoyed the challenge it presented and it raised the standards of fielding and players' fitness to new heights. It also introduced the game to new fans, especially in Australia. It has become so popular that it underwrites the more traditional variety of the game and is an established and essential part of it. But the administrators need to examine ways of properly marrying the two to ensure that one does not dominate to the detriment of the other.

One upshot of World Series Cricket was the introduction of helmets as an accepted part of the gear. I've seen old pictures of West Indians and Indians batting in pith helmets but that was protection from the sun, not from the bowling. The Australians in the West Indies in 1965 reportedly sent back home for helmets to counteract the threat of Wes Hall and Charlie Griffith and were derided for it. The view then was that there was something 'sissy' about it, that it showed a lack of courage. The fact that the world's fastest bowlers were lined up against him in World Series Cricket influenced Dennis Amiss to be the first to bite the bullet and don a helmet. The rest soon followed and now very few go to the wicket without one. Viv Richards was a notable exception and Richie Richardson follows his example.

I can well understand the desire for batsmen to protect themselves against injury. This is the age of fast bowling and dodgy pitches and one mistake leading to a blow to the head or face can end a man's professional career – or worse. I wore one myself although I seldom stayed around long enough to have it tested.

The fault I place on the helmet is that it gives batsmen a false sense of security. With it on, they feel they can do anything without getting hurt. This is where the basic skills of handling fast bowling are lost. The need always to watch the ball and to get into line is absent. You don't see many batsmen bobbing and weaving out of the way of the bouncer or riding it while slackening the wrists to keep it down. Nor are there many really good hookers these days. Those skills seem to have been lost and helmets have played a detrimental part in the process. It appears to be a strange contradiction that more batsmen are being hit using helmets and that more catches are being taken at short-leg. Batsmen who are wearing elaborate protective gear don't see the need to learn to evade bouncers and are too weighed down to be able to hook properly. It is pertinent that two of the best hookers, Richards and Richardson, have never used helmets and have very seldom been hit. There are other reasons for it, such as the decline in the standard of pitches and the prevalence of fast bowling, but I am sure helmets have contributed to a deterioration of technique.

Coinciding with the arrival of the helmet, but with no direct connection that I can see, came the change in batting stance. It entailed lifting the bat high off the ground as the bowler ran in, rather than keeping it on the crease in the traditional manner. Tony Greig, who at least had some excuse as he was 6 feet 5 inches tall, initiated it and was followed by some English batsmen and a few from other countries. I'm happy to say, none were West Indian. The theory sounds fine. Since you eventually have to pick up your bat in any case to make a stroke, why not save the time and have it up already as the bowler delivers? The answer to that is simply provided by the records of all the great players who, for balance and coordination, kept their bats down before going into their stroke.

I suppose those who use it respond that each player must work out what he is most comfortable with and the raised-bat stance has been successful for some, its best advertisement being Graham Gooch. I can only say that I was encouraged when I saw the fellow at the opposite end waiting for me to deliver with his bat held high off the ground. I always felt it was more likely to get through. It gave me a psychological advantage and that's the last thing a batsman wants to concede to the bowler.

Pitches have come in for increasing criticism and I believe it is generally justified in the countries in which I played most, the West Indies, Australia and England. When I first went to Australia, only Melbourne was not up to scratch but that was a problem, I was told, associated with the amount of Australian rules football played on the ground during the wet winters. It got no better and was joined as below par by the pitch at the Sydney Cricket Ground, which used to be true and even but developed, or probably was allowed to develop, into a raging turner, conditions which led to our successive defeats there in the 1984–85 and 1988–89 series. Sabina Park in Jamaica was rightly described as a 'horror strip' by the English tabloids when Mike Gatting got knocked over and his team-mates were frightened out of their wits on England's tour of 1986. It remained unpredictable for some years but there are signs that it is now regaining its former status as one of the best in the world. The Queen's Park Oval in Trinidad is certainly not ideal for Test cricket and some of those I played on in the county championship in England and in regional matches in the West Indies were nothing short of diabolical. It reached the stage when that match between Derbyshire and Nottinghamshire in 1989 had to be abandoned because the pitch was unplayable (see Chapter 23). That was at Trent Bridge which was once rated as the best batting wicket in England.

The pitch is one of the most important components of the game. It dictates the level of play, indeed whether there will be any at all. Without good pitches, there can't be good cricket or good cricketers. If you're playing on surfaces from which one ball is exploding off a length and the next is skidding through low, you don't know where you are. Batsmen can't play each ball on its merits. It makes batting nothing more than a lottery and cricketers cannot develop properly.

As a bowler, it may be asked, why should I complain? Yet I am sure most bowlers prefer bowling on good pitches, with even pace and predictable bounce. I certainly did because I knew what the ball was going to do and how to adjust accordingly. If I didn't know how much bounce to expect or how much movement, control became very difficult. The target area for a bowler is so small that any adjustments need to be minor. A couple of inches wider of off stump or shorter in length, you expect the ball to behave a little bit differently. On some well-grassed surfaces in England, the problem was that it did too much. A delivery on what would normally be a good line just outside the off stump would move so much that the batsman could leave it alone. Trying to compensate with a middle-stump line would only produce a straight ball or else one that flew down the leg side if the seam hit the grass differently. The same is true with variable bounce, when one ball dug in short sails over the batsman's head and the next, pitched on the same length, keeps down around the knees. That makes control impossible for the bowler, strokeplay uncertain for the batsman, and the cricket unsatisfactory.

Many of Australia's Test players in the last twenty years have been produced by Western Australia, and many of our great cricketers in the West Indies have come from Barbados and, more recently, Antigua. The common denominator is the type of pitch on which they were reared. Those at the WACA ground in Perth, at Kensington Oval in Bridgetown and the Recreation Ground in St. John's were true and even in their pace and bounce with excellent sighting. The environment was ideal for cricket.

I personally don't know enough about soil and the preparation of pitches to suggest what can be done to reach an international standard. I've heard those who claim to be experts say that, like human beings, squares age and develop wrinkles and warts. They need an occasional face-lift through digging up or turning over. Judging by what happened at Sabina Park, I am not convinced that is the solution.

It is a vital area to which not much attention has been paid. It has become a problem and it needs attention now from the authorities at all levels. The stage has been reached in England where a pitch inspector was appointed and points deducted from teams with sub-standard pitches. It was a severe measure but it appears to have worked.

Even more than the arguments over one-day cricket, fast bowling, helmets and pitches, three main issues threw the game into unpleasantness and discord during my eleven years as a Test player – Kerry Packer, South Africa and umpiring. Packer quickly passed although his legacy remains. South Africa now seems to be finally settled. Even though the International Cricket Council (ICC) has finally agreed in principle to the appointment of an international panel of umpires, it still has to be implemented.

The preceding pages document my run-ins with umpires in sufficient detail to leave no doubt about my support for such a panel. Everyone accepts that umpires, being human, will make mistakes but players, also being human, are more liable to accept them as genuine if they know the umpires are not connected in any way to either team. We would certainly not have had the trouble we did in New Zealand in 1980, and there would not have been the repeated unpleasantness generated on so many tours down through the years, had there been independent umpires.

I am still unaware of how the ICC would select their panel. If it is to be the best, they'll end up with two-thirds of them English umpires simply because the English, generally speaking, are the best. They are the only ones who do the job on a daily basis, so they get more practice than anyone else. The great majority are former players, giving them the advantage too of practical experience. But would it be equitable to have the panel dominated by one country? Other sports have long since overcome that particular problem and it is high time cricket does the same. We have waited too long.

CHAPTER 25

Me and the horses

My love affair with horse-racing is as long and as strong as that with cricket.

Even before I played schools cricket, I was up mornings cutting grass from the piece of land out back of our place on Dunrobin Avenue with my brother Ralph, and then being driven to the race track at Caymanas Park on the outskirts of Kingston to deliver it to Mrs Skeffrey's horses. Mrs Skeffrey was a nurse, our next-door neighbour and close friend of the family. She was also Ralph's godmother which was enough to qualify him for the job of cutting grass – and his younger brother for helping him.

The magnificent thoroughbreds I saw immediately fascinated me but, as boys do at that age, I lost interest as cricket and football occupied my time and energy. It wasn't until I was in the third form at Kingston College that my interest in horses was rekindled by some classmates who seemed to know everything there was to know about the local racing scene. Not wanting to sound ignorant on matters such as who was the better trainer of Billy Williams and Laurie Silvera or the better jockey of Kenneth Mattis and Winston Ellis, I started to go out to Caymanas on race days with Kemp Skeffrey, nurse Skeffrey's son. Eventually I got to know just about everything as well and was even nicknamed 'Tempus' for a while at school after a horse at Caymanas in which

I had more faith than his form merited. I was hooked and have been ever since.

I love horses and every aspect of racing. I was lucky that through my cricket travels and contacts I could see so much of it in the great racing and breeding countries of the world, England, Australia and New Zealand. I visited stud farms wherever I went simply to touch the horses, to see them frolicking and galloping around the paddock or even doing no more than standing around grazing. I am always struck by the impressive combination of their power and their grace and enthralled when they put it to the test of competition on the track.

It was inevitable that I would get into racing myself and I had a few horses in Jamaica before I sold out in October 1985. I owned a colt by the name of Bunny's Halo in partnership with Andrew Nunes and leased two others, Undercover and Precocious, with Howard Hamilton, an old friend who, as head of the Shell oil company in Jamaica, had a lot to do with Shield cricket. It was a fairly successful operation and Undercover, whose sire, Secret Man, was a top performer in England, won quite a few races. But being away from Jamaica so often playing cricket meant I wasn't getting much fun out of it and I decided to sell up. I was also concerned that too many odd little things were happening in Jamaican racing at the time. There was doping and charges that races were being fixed. I didn't appreciate paying training fees to have other people do what they wanted with my horses, so I decided to get out.

Having spent so much time in England, I got to know more and more people involved in racing which eventually led to Michael Stoute and Newmarket. Michael is a Barbadian who went to England just after leaving school and eventually rose to become one of the top trainers in the country, training for the Aga Khan and other famous owners. The great Derby winner, Shergar, was in his stable. I was introduced to him by a fellow Barbadian, Ronald Burke, himself a trainer whom I'd got to know through my Jamaican racing contacts, and we became good friends. Michael is mad on cricket, so there was plenty for us to talk about besides racing. I spent many happy hours with him at his place in Newmarket, going up to the heath to watch the horses exercise, chatting with his head lad, Jimmy Scott, and stable jockey, Wally Swinburn, and soaking up the atmosphere in the heart of the horse-racing business in England. I even turned out in the occasional Sunday match for his team of trainers and jockeys.

Paradoxically, I didn't go on race days much in England. I preferred to stay at home and follow the TV coverage from which I could take in everything from the parade ring, all through the race to the finish with slow-motion replays as a bonus. At the track you don't actually see much of the horses, which is my real pleasure. You do get a good look in the parade ring but then they disappear into the distance and the next time you see them is thundering down the home-stretch. The fun at the track is the atmosphere and the ambience, chatting to a trainer, a jockey or a head lad, not seeing the horses flash past the winning post. On the TV, I could study the tactics of the jockeys and the actions of the horses. I found that more entertaining.

I've won some money and lost some to totes and bookmakers over the years but I wouldn't rate myself a big gambler by any means or a compulsive one. Horse-racing and cricketers seem to go hand-in-hand, certainly in the Caribbean. Wes Hall, Sir Gary Sobers, Charlie Griffith, Seymour Nurse and Peter Lashley are all Test players from the 1960s who have been involved in Barbados, either as owners or Turf Club officials.

Joey Carew, another of the 1960s Test clan, is big in the sport in Trinidad. And there are not many cricket dressing-rooms where you won't find someone poring over the tips in the day's paper or on the phone to his bookie.

Some even turn it to their advantage. When we toured Australia in 1981–82, Harold Joseph was the lone spinner in the team. He was a jovial Trinidadian who found that our selection policy allowed him plenty of time to indulge his favourite pastime of betting on the proliferation of race meetings they have in Australia. He only played a couple of matches but 'Joe-Joe' was doing too well on the horses to let that worry him too much. 'I catch them again,' we would hear him say, big grin on his face, and we'd know he'd backed another winner.

A lot of cricketers take a day at the races for relaxation. I never did it for that reason. I would come back from the track and head straight for bed, mentally and physically exhausted, perhaps because I was so thoroughly involved. But it did take my mind completely off cricket.

When my playing days were over and I returned to Jamaica, I got back into racing. Now that I'm more or less settled, I hope to get into breeding, an interesting side of the business. I've bought a filly of excellent pedigree and expect she'll produce offspring of good enough quality to be attractive to buyers.

My other hobbies, such as they are, don't extend much beyond watching television and listening to music. Television gradually took the place of the movies which I frequented in my youth. I soon found that, contrary to what seems a widely held notion, the life of the professional cricketer doesn't allow much free time. A typical playing day entails being at the ground at least an hour before the start, in other words around 9 a.m. for Test cricket, and getting back to the team's hotel about an hour after play, at around 6.30 p.m. (or later in England).

When I had a hard day in the field I wanted to relax and unwind. While others had different ways, I was quite content going to my room, ordering a room service meal and watching whatever was on offer on the TV. With satellite channels and videos available in even the remotest town, there was usually something worthwhile. If there wasn't, a selection from my music tapes would suffice. I usually carried a wide selection of reggae, calypso or soul wherever I went which helped take cricket off my mind for a while. I wasn't too much of a party person and preferred to accept invitations for a meal at home rather than head for the nearest disco.

That was my way of taking things easy. Others had theirs. To each his own, so long as it doesn't affect performance. The game is full of legendary tales of the nocturnal activities of many of the great players and there were a few in my time who enjoyed life to the full. I had neither the inclination nor the energy to expend dancing the night away when I faced the prospect of bowling twenty overs the next day.

CHAPTER 26

Looking to the future

Cricket has been my life and it's been good to me.

If there is one thing I'd do differently if I had the chance to press the rewind button, I would train harder. When I was young, I didn't put in the work that I came to know is necessary to bowl fast at the highest level. I did most of my training at Kingston College for athletics, not for cricket, so that when I got into the Jamaica team I was embarrassingly unfit. Perhaps if I'd done as much preparation as I should have in the early days I would not have been plagued by injury quite as frequently as I was.

I am satisfied that I quit at the right time. A lot of sportsmen make the decision, find they can't live with it and hanker to get back into action. 'They never come back' is one of sport's oldest and truest maxims and I'm glad I haven't had the urge to try. If anything, I believe I carried on a little too long.

It was exciting while it lasted. It took time to get used to the travelling and the inevitable homesickness of being away for such long periods. The tour of Australia in 1975–76 was a traumatic introduction to the big time but it wasn't long before firm friendships developed with several team-mates, friendships that I'm sure will last as long as I live. I was caught up in the thrill of being part of a successful and closely-knit team in which we enjoyed each other's company. While we might all have been dying to get back home after a lengthy tour, a short lay-off would be enough to stoke the anticipation for the next one as much for the cricket as for the comradeship of being together. Little things like horsing around over a Chinese takeaway with a bunch of guys in someone's room or listening to the old jokes always raised a laugh.

I have always kept a photograph of the great George Headley presenting me with a trophy while I was at Kingston College. He was quite a small man with a soft-spoken way about him but he was revered in Jamaica. On the back of the photo, George Headley wrote: 'Play cricket and see the world. This should be an inspiration to achieve the maximum of attainments of your choice.' So it proved.

As time went on, the excitement gradually waned. It was no doubt one of the symptoms of the passing years. I had increasing responsibilities at home and more and more of those in the team with whom I was closest were leaving. It became harder and harder to sustain energy and enthusiasm and, when I ceased to enjoy it, I knew the time had come for the final curtain call.

Since then, I have had to change the direction of my life. Professional sportsmen are almost unique in that they have to end their careers in the prime of life when their counterparts in most other professions are steadily climbing the ladder, not about to step off. My heart is still very much in cricket although I don't miss the playing side of it at all.

Immediately on retiring, I was elected to the management committee of Melbourne Club and to the Jamaica Cricket Association board of management. I helped prepare, and select, the Jamaica youth team which won the 1990 regional championship and have also been involved with the senior Jamaica team for the Red Stripe Cup.

Jamaica and West Indies cricket has been administered over the years mainly by ex-Test players. The last three Presidents of the West Indies Board have been three of our top batsmen of the 1950s, the late Jeffrey Stollmeyer of Trinidad, Allan Rae of Jamaica, and now Clyde Walcott, one of the celebrated Three Ws, from Barbados. That is as it should be. Those who have played the game at the highest level have more of a feel of it and can usually relate to the players' point of view. The game has given me a great deal of pleasure and satisfaction, quite apart from being my profession, and I am eager to put something back into it, to try to help maintain standards in Jamaica and West Indies cricket. I have even given thought to taking up umpiring but, realistically, I do not think I would have sufficient time for that. Whatever the future holds, I am sure cricket will be part of it.

When I stopped playing, I still had to earn my daily crust and that meant finding a job. Like all cricketers, I was spoiled by the lifestyle I had enjoyed for seventeen years and I couldn't bear the thought of working in an office with the regimen of punchclock times. I'm too much of an outdoor person for that. I took the first step from cricketer to businessman by buying out a Shell service station in the commercial district of New Kingston which meant I was my own boss. My friends tell me I should be able to manage my time so that I have more of it to myself. They say I should delegate authority. That is easier said than done for a business that opens from 7 a.m. to 11 p.m. But I'm excited by the challenge just as I am by the challenge of getting into coaching and trying to spot young talent and bring it along. It's now a matter of combining the two.

I've also got into radio and television commentaries

and enjoy it immensely. It has kept me in touch with the game and given me a different perspective on it. It's an area that has provided a comfortable living for several ex-players of whom the outstanding example is Richie Benaud, the former Australian captain who has made such a reputation for himself on television in England and Australia. The scope is much more limited in the Caribbean than elsewhere because our radio and TV stations are so small, but Trans-World International's (TWI) live ball-by-ball coverage of the last three series in the West Indies involving England, Australia and South Africa shows the possibilities. Thankfully, I've found I was able to accept a contract from Channel 9 to do the 1992–93 series in Australia. But in future it's going to be difficult. In Jamaica, a service station needs careful financial management since there is such a small profit margin on petrol sales, only six per cent. It would be foolish to expect things to fall into place right away and I'll wait to see how they work out.

Even living full-time back in Jamaica took a little getting used to. There was not a year during my international career when I didn't spend at least three months away. Often, it was six months and more. Perhaps, now that my playing days are over, I'll be able to settle into a more lasting relationship than the three I've had, none of which survived. My only marriage ended in divorce and two other partnerships broke up, each producing a child, all of whom live with their mothers. My thirteen-year-old daughter, Melinda, is in New York, my eleven-year-old son, Ryan Marc, in Australia, and my three-year-old daughter, Tiana, is in Jamaica. The nomadic existence of a cricketer places a great strain on any relationship, but life goes on.

One aspect of my personal life that has remained strong and constant is the support I receive from my closely-knit family. I was the baby, the last of four children, the one usually spoiled. But my parents spoiled all of us, if that means always trying to get the best for their children and sacrificing to do so. When I first showed an aptitude for cricket, my father made sure it was encouraged without ever being overbearing about it. If my mother was not at first one hundred per cent behind the idea of me becoming a professional cricketer, she fully backed me once I had made the decision. My father travelled to Australia to see me play my first Test in Brisbane and remained throughout the series. He then brought along Mum for the following series in England. It was an inspiration and a comfort to know that they cared so much and I know that, wherever my life leads me, they will continue to be by my side.

Throughout my career, I was encouraged, at times almost embarrassed, by the wholehearted support I got from the people of Jamaica and the West Indies. I appreciated the exalted place cricket held in our society and the reason for it and realised that those of us who made it to the top were more than ordinary sportsmen. We were national heroes and role models. I always felt a great sense of responsibility representing Jamaica and the West Indies, conscious of the effect our performances would have on West Indians everywhere.

C.L.R. James explained it perfectly in his *Beyond a Boundary*. 'West Indians crowding to Tests bring with them the whole past history and future hopes of the islands. English people, for example, have a conception of themselves breathed from birth. Drake and the mighty Nelson, Shakespeare, Waterloo, the Charge of the Light Brigade, the few who did so much for so many, the success of parliamentary democracy, those and such as those constitute a national tradition. Underdeveloped countries have to go back centuries to rebuild one. We of the West Indies have none at all, none that we know of. To such people the three Ws, Ram and Val wrecking English batting, help to fill a huge gap in their consciousness and their needs.' A packed Sabina Park, chanting 'Mikey, Mikey' as I ran in to bowl, was all the inspiration any fast bowler needed.

On my retirement, I was touched by the many tributes that came my way and by a special testimonial match held in my honour by Melbourne in which Clive Lloyd, Andy Roberts, Joel Garner, Roy Fredericks and Wes Hall all played. At a lunch hosted by Jamaica's Minister of Youth and Community Development, Ed Bartlett, the emotion became too much and, midway through my reply to the many speeches, I broke down in tears and couldn't continue.

During the relatively short period of my playing career, I witnessed so many fundamental changes to the game that I can't imagine what will be next. There is a danger that the amount of cricket being played will devalue it and that the players will become burnt out before their time. South Africa's return and Zimbabwe's addition to the list of Test teams compounds the issue. The ideal would be to reduce the number of Tests and one-day internationals but that would mean losing revenue in broadcasting rights and sponsorship that keep the game running. And what player would voluntarily take a rest if he had a generous offer put to him to play somewhere else? It's a dilemma I can't see the administrators solving.

Our biggest problem in the West Indies, certainly in Jamaica, is the declining standards of our club competitions from which we get our future stars. The exodus of our best players on pro contracts in Britain and even Holland during the summer months has diluted the strength of the club game, leaving mediocrity in their wake. A look at almost all the Red Stripe Cup teams shows that more than seventy per cent of the players are out of their countries for the better part of the club seasons. When I first played Senior Cup cricket in Jamaica, I was among two or three schoolboys good enough to make it at that level. Now there are twenty or so, some not good enough even to play for their schools, just making up numbers. It means the competitive edge is gone and it requires less talent, and less commitment, to get into the Jamaican team.

Not only have standards dropped but so has public interest. Back in the 1970s, when I was first coming into the game, we would expect a couple of thousand spectators for a big club match in Jamaica between Melbourne and Kensington. The same thing obtained in Barbados and Guyana. Now we get a few hundred at most. That is another problem with no obvious solution. There is no professional club cricket in the Caribbean, so players will continue to head off in their numbers to where they can sell their talents and gain international experience. It is a route that I and hundreds of others have taken over the years.

The best answer is simply to keep on producing players of the quality and in the quantity that maintain our standard at the top.

I intend to be involved in the process.

Statistical appendix

Michael Holding's career figures

TEST AND FIRST-CLASS CRICKET

Season	Team	Opponents	Venue	M	I	NO	RUNS	HS	AVGE	100s	50s	CT	OV	MD	RUNS	Wkts	AVGE	BB
									BATTING								**BOWLING**	
1972-73	Jamaica	Shell Shield	IIs	3	5		33	15	6.60				67	13	217	5	43.40	
1972-73	Jamaica	Australian Tourist	WI	1	2		9	9	4.50				23	6	69	2	34.50	
1972-73	WI President's XI	Australian Tourist	WI	1	2	1	1	1	1.00			1	18	1	59	1	59.00	
1973-74	Jamaica	Shell Shield	IIs	2	1		1	1	1.00			1	48	7	162	1	162.00	
1973-74	WI President's XI	M.C.C. Tourist	WI	1	2		6	5	3.00			1	7	2	14	0		
1974-75	Jamaica	Shell Shield	IIs	4	5	1	44	*32	11.00			1	93.3	19	297	7	42.42	
1975-76	West Indies	Tour of Australia	A	2	4	1	131	62	43.66		2	1	56	5	212	9	23.55	
1975-76	West Indies	Australia Tests	A	5	9		95	34	10.55			3	140.5	15	614	10	61.40	
1975-76	West Indies	India Tests	WI	4	6	1	77	55	15.40		1		138	35	378	19	19.89	
1976	West Indies	Tour of England	E	8	8	1	111	42	15.85			5	180.2	57	435	27	16.11	
1976	West Indies	England Tests	E	4	5		41	32	8.20				159.3	54	356	28	12.71	
1976-77	Jamaica	Shell Shield	IIs	1	2	1	33	*33	33.00			1	10	3	18	1	18.00	
1977-78	Jamaica	Australian Tourist	WI	1	2		28	17	14.00			2	35.2	8	83	7	11.85	
1979-80	West Indies	Tour of Australia	A	1	1		2	2	2.00				29	8	88	4	22.00	
1979-80	West Indies	Australia Tests	A	3	4	1	22	11	7.33			2	111	24	319	14	22.78	
1979-80	West Indies	Tour of New Zealand	NZ	1	2		5	5	2.50				26	6	61	1	61.00	
1979-80	West Indies	New Zealand Tests	NZ	3	5	1	28	*16	7.00				94	21	236	7	33.70	
1979-80	Jamaica	Shell Shield	IIs	1	2	1	14	*10	14.00			2	43	9	134	5	26.80	
1980	West Indies	Tour of England	E	6	5	2	38	20	12.66				161.2	40	464	24	19.33	
1980	West Indies	England Tests	E	5	6	4	61	35	30.50			1	230.5	56	632	20	31.60	
1980-81	West Indies	Tour of Pakistan	P	3	3		24	19	8.00				57	12	169	6	28.16	
1980-81	Jamaica	Shell Shield	IIs	4	5		51	33	10.20				99	13	332	13	25.53	
1980-81	West Indies	England Tests	WI	4	4	1	84	*58	28.00		1	1	132.2	38	315	17	18.52	
1981	Lancashire	Counties	E	7	8	2	66	32	11.00			2	271.1	75	715	40	17.87	
1981-82	International XI	Tour of Pakistan	P	2	4	1	131	67	43.66		1		46.1	11	144	8	18.00	
1981-82	West Indies	Tour of Australia	A	3	2		30	24	15.00			1	70	12	191	8	23.87	
1981-82	West Indies	Australia Tests	A	3	5		26	9	5.20			2	140.3	37	344	24	14.33	
1982-83	West Indies XI	International XI	WI	1	1	1	3	*3					14	5	33	0		
1982-83	Tasmania	Sheffield Shield	A	9	11	2	187	*47	20.77			3	371.4	93	946	36	26.27	
1982-83	Jamaica	Shell Shield	IIs	1	2		22	16	11.00			1	34.2	7	139	3	46.33	
1982-83	West Indies	India Tests	WI	5	5		27	24	5.40			3	162	23	502	12	41.83	

Season	Team	Competition	v	M	I	NO	Runs	HS	Avge	100	50	Ct	O	Mdn	R	W	Avge	Best
1983-84	West Indies	India Tests					141	56	20.14			1	223.4	43	663	30	22.10	
1983-84	West Indies	Australia Tests	WI	6	3		3	*3	3.00				101.5	20	245	13	18.84	
1984	West Indies	Tour of England	E	3	2		31	31	15.50			1	56.3	18	143	6	23.83	
1984	West Indies	England Tests	E	4	5		158	69	31.60			2	122.2	24	343	15	22.86	
1984-85	West Indies	Tour of Australia	A	3	3		47	21	15.66			4	80.2	20	161	5	32.20	
1984-85	West Indies	Australia Tests	A	3	4		2	1	0.50			2	81.1	20	249	15	16.60	
1984-85	West Indies	New Zealand Tests	WI	3	3		21	12	7.00			1	82	24	218	9	24.22	
1985	Derbyshire	Counties	E	12	19		413	80	22.94		3	6	354.5	67	1124	50	22.48	
1985-86	Jamaica	Shell Shield	IIs	5	9		114	34	12.66			7	77	17	251	15	16.73	
1985-86	Jamaica	English Tourist	WI	1	D								13.3	1	44	2	22.00	
1985-86	West Indies	England Tests	WI	4	4		124	73	31.00		1	3	102.4	16	385	16	24.06	
1986	Derbyshire	Counties	E	14	20		295	*36	16.38			6	388.1	110	1045	52	20.09	
1986-87	West Indies	Tour of Australia	A	1	1		2	2	2.00			1	11	3	18	3	6.00	
1986-87	West Indies	Tour of New Zealand	NZ	1	1		34	*34				2	34	6	104	4	26.00	
1986-87	West Indies	New Zealand Tests	NZ	1	1		0	0				1	37	8	99	0		
1986-87	Jamaica	Shell Shield	IIs	2	3		4	4	1.33			1	56	10	157	12	13.08	
1986-87	Jamaica	Lancashire Tourist XI	WI	1	D								7	2	12	0		
1987	Derbyshire	Counties	E	13	18		278	*63	17.37		1	10	391.2	72	1194	49	24.36	
1987-88	Canterbury	N.Z. Shell Shield	NZ	7	11		62	31	8.85			9	258.5	90	488	29	16.82	
1987-88	Jamaica	Red Stripe Cup	IIs	2	2		30	24	30.00				45	8	140	7	20.00	
1988	Derbyshire	Counties	E	11	12		129	*30	12.90			7	279.1	49	827	24	34.45	
1988-89	Jamaica	Red Stripe Cup	IIs	5	7		71	15	11.83			11	92	15	268	10	26.80	
1989	Derbyshire	Counties	E	10	13		90	34	10.00			8	258	46	863	28	30.82	
	Jamaica			34	47	5	454	34	10.80			29	743.4	138	2323	90	25.81	
	West Indies			97	115	17	1405	73	14.33		8	42	2893.1	663	8113	351	23.11	
	Derbyshire			66	87	12	1295	80	17.26		5	39	1840.3	385	5504	224	24.57	
	Lancashire			7	8	2	66	32	11.00			2	271.1	75	715	40	17.87	
	Tasmania			9	11	2	187	*47	20.77			3	371.4	93	946	36	26.27	
	Canterbury			7	11	4	62	31	8.85			9	258.5	90	488	29	16.82	
	International XI			2	4	1	131	67	43.66		1	1	46.1	11	144	8	18.00	
	Test Record			60	76	10	910	73	13.78	0	6	22	2058.4	458	5898	249	23.68	8-92
	Career			222	283	43	3600	80	15.00	0	14	125	6425.1	1455	18233	778	22.43	8-92

ONE-DAY INTERNATIONALS

			BATTING					BOWLING				
Season	Opp. or tournament	No. match pld	Innings	Not outs	Runs	Highest Score	AVGE	Overs	Maidens	Runs	Wickets	AVGE	Runs/over
1976	England	3	2		19	16	9.50	26.0	2	98	2	49.00	3.76
1979	World Cup	4	1		0	0	0.00	41.0	5	106	8	13.25	2.58
1979-80	WSC	9	5	1	15	8	3.75	83.4	10	291	12	24.25	3.48
1980	N. Zealand	1						9.4	1	23	1	23.00	2.44
1980	England	2	2		0	0	0.00	20.0	3	44	5	8.88	2.20
1980	Pakistan	1						5.3	3	5	1	5.00	0.90
1981	England	1	1		1	1	1.00	16.2	1	43	3	14.33	2.62
1981-82	WSC	13	7	2	31	18	6.20	118.0	15	390	19	20.52	3.30
1983	India	3	1		2	2	2.00	20.4	3	73	2	36.50	3.54
1983	World Cup	7	4	1	36	20	12.00	74.5	11	236	12	18.40	2.86
1983-84	India	4	1	1	0	0*	0.00	27.0	4	94	3	31.33	3.48
1984	WSC	12	5	2	79	64	19.75	113.3	9	411	23	17.86	3.62
1984	Australia	2						18.0	0	101	1	101.00	5.61
1984-85	WSC	12	2	1	3	2*	3.00	120.0	8	443	16	27.68	3.69
1984	England	3	2	1	12	12*	12.00	30.5	3	85	6	14.16	2.76
1985	N. Zealand	5	1		9	9	9.00	34.0	4	95	5	19.00	2.79
1985	Sharjah	2						14.0	3	45	2	22.50	3.21
1985	Pakistan	5	2		2	2	1.00	35.1	2	153	9	17.00	4.34
1985	WSC	4	1		5	5	5.00	30.0	3	75	3	25.00	2.50
1986	England	2	1	1	0	0*	0.00	19.0	2	61	2	30.50	3.21
1987	WSC & Perth CS	6	4	1	65	53*	21.66	54.3	4	162	7	23.14	2.97

TOTAL MATCHES: 102

BATTING: 42 innings, 11 not-outs, 279 runs, highest score 64 v. Australia, Perth, 1984; average 9.00.

BOWLING: 911.4 overs, 102 maidens, 3,034 runs, 142 wickets, average 21.36.

Best figures 5–26 v. Australia, Sydney, 1985. Runs per over 3.32.